Architect's Job Book
Sixth edition 1995

Architect's

Job Book

Sixth edition 1995

RIBA Publications

Architect's Job Book
Sixth edition 1995

Editors: Stanley Cox and Alaine Hamilton

© RIBA Publications 1995
ISBN 1 85946 007 0

Published by RIBA Publications, a Division of RIBA Companies Ltd,
Finsbury Mission, 39 Moreland Street, London EC1V 8BB

Book design: Mike Stribbling
Design team: Mike Stribbling, Gordon Burrows, Philip Handley

Typesetting by Trevor Gray Typography, Wisbech, Cambs

Printed and bound by Butler and Tanner Ltd, Frome, Somerset

Foreword

By Owen Luder, President of the Royal Institute of British Architects

Architecture is not just about flair and imagination. It is also the demanding and at times tedious process of translating design into a finished building with a satisfied client.

So successful architects are those who organise themselves to systematically translate their imagination and design flair into a building that meets their clients' needs. Finished on time within budget!

The need for this systematic approach to the design and construction process was recognised when in 1969 the first very successful edition of the *Architect's Job Book* was published.

Since then much has changed.

Clients' procurements methods, building technology and forms of contract have all changed dramatically. Competitive fees leave no margin for inefficiency. The ever present risk of negligence claims means no architect can risk errors or omissions.

All architects must adopt and keep updated clear and consistent systems to deal with all aspects of the design and building process.

This new edition of the *Architect's Job Book* provides the framework for this systematic approach, which can be applied to any building or procurement method.

An essential *aide-mémoire* for all practising architects.

October 1995

Editors' Notes

Sixth edition

When the *Architect's Job Book* was first published in 1969 it took as its framework the RIBA Plan of Work, which has become widely recognised in the construction industry and its associated professions as a model set of procedures for job administration. In this sixth edition, the Plan of Work structure is retained, although the content has been completely revised and updated. The Job Book has reverted to a single volume concerned with job administration, and the detail of contract administration peculiar to specific forms of building contract is covered in other titles from RIBA Publications.

The reality of architectural practice today is that there is no one predominant method of procurement. Although this Job Book is arranged in a form which is obviously applicable to traditional procurement, sound job administration procedures are equally necessary with Design and Build or Management procurement, and this is recognised in the checklists and references.

Standard forms

Since publication of the fifth edition in 1988, the number and range of standard forms of building contract and consultants' appointing documents has greatly increased. This new edition of the Job Book has been written mainly with users of JCT 80, IFC 84 and MW 80 in mind. However both Design and Build and Management procurement are covered, with references to JCT CD 81 (With Contractor's Design) and to the JCT MC 87 (Management Contract).

In 1992, *Architect's Appointment* was replaced by the SFA/92 series of appointing documents, augmented in 1995 by the Conditions of Engagement (CE/95) suitable for smaller and less complex commissions. The documents referred to in the Job Book are listed in the References and Further Reading at the end of the book.

Terminology

In this edition the terminology used when referring to the development of the brief accords with BS 7000 part 4; that used in relation to Work Stages refers to the RIBA Plan of Work; and references to Quality Management accord with the RIBA's *Quality Management: Guidance for an Office Manual*, and BS 5750.

The CDM Regulations

Health and safety legislation has been extended with the coming into force of the Construction (Design and Management) Regulations 1994. The importance of the 'CDM Regs' both to the architect acting as Designer and to the architect appointed as Planning Supervisor is reflected in the checklists. Where an architect acts as Planning Supervisor under a separate appointment the RIBA Form of Appointment PS/95 has been taken as the model document.

Quality management

Whether or not it is pursued to the status of Quality Assurance, quality management is viewed as evidence of sound practice in the 1990s. The Job Book includes recurring references to the project quality plan in the Stage-related checklists. It is also possible to adapt the Job Book itself to form a quality plan document.

It is accepted that today's architects may not always be appointed initially to take a job through the complete Plan of Work Stages. There will be many instances where the appointment will proceed on a Stage by Stage basis, or may even be for part of a Stage. Pragmatism and flexibility are needed in architectural practice in the 1990s and the sixth edition recognises this: while setting out systematic procedures for job administration it offers advice that is sound, helpful and realistic.

Contents

Foreword
Editors' Notes
List of Figures

Page 11   **Pre-Agreement**

PRE/1   Professional services
PRE/2   Actions
PRE/3   Watchpoints
PRE/4   Action checks

Supplement
PRE/S1   Practice statement
PRE/S2   Selection of an architect
PRE/S3   Appointment of architect as lead consultant
PRE/S4   Appointment of architect as consultant in design and build
PRE/S5   Appointment of architect as project manager
PRE/S6   Appointment of architect as construction manager
PRE/S7   Appointment of architect as Planning Supervisor

35   **A–B**   **Inception and Feasibility**

A–B/1   Activities
A–B/2   Actions
A–B/3   Stage summary
A–B/4   Watchpoints
A–B/5   Action checks

Supplement
A–B/S1   The briefing process
A–B/S2   Project brief checklist
A–B/S3   Design team appointments and working
A–B/S4   Planning permission, other consents and approvals
A–B/S5   Health and safety checklists
A–B/S6   A project quality plan
A–B/S7   Inspecting the site
A–B/S8   Financial appraisal

73   **C**   **Outline Proposals**

C/1   Activities
C/2   Actions
C/3   Stage summary
C/4   Watchpoints
C/5   Action checks

Supplement
C/S1   Design and build documentation
C/S2   Design brief: checklist
C/S3   Design team roles

Contents

Page 91   **D**   **Scheme Design**

D/1   Activities
D/2   Actions
D/3   Stage summary
D/4   Watchpoints
D/5   Action checks

Supplement
D/S1   Scheme design presentation
D/S2   Design team roles

107   **E**   **Detail Design**

E/1   Activities
E/2   Actions
E/3   Stage summary
E/4   Watchpoints
E/5   Action checks

Supplement
E/S1   Design information: Implications of procurement method
E/S2   Procedures for the issue of drawings
E/S3   Design team roles

131   **F–G**   **Production Information and Bills of Quantities**

F–G/1   Activities
F–G/2   Actions
F–G/3   Stage summary
F–G/4   Watchpoints
F–G/5   Action checks

Supplement
F–G/S1   Production information
F–G/S2   Production information: Specification and Schedules of work
F–G/S3   Production information: Bills of quantities
F–G/S4   Building control approval checklist
F–G/S5   Design team roles

153   **H**   **Tender Action**

H/1   Activities
H/2   Actions
H/3   Stage summary
H/4   Watchpoints
H/5   Action checks

Supplement
H/S1   Selective tendering lists
H/S2   Selective tendering: Specialist subcontractors and suppliers
H/S3   Selective tendering: Main contract – Traditional procurement
H/S4   Selective tendering: Main contract – Design and build procurement
H/S5   Selective tendering: Main contract – Management procurement

Contents

Page 183   **J**   **Project Planning**

J/1   Activities
J/2   Actions
J/3   Stage summary
J/4   Watchpoints
J/5   Action checks

Supplement
J/S1   Dealing with the contract documents
J/S2   Site inspectorate appointment and briefing
J/S3   Initial project team meeting
J/S4   Insurances check

213   **K–L**   **Operations on Site and Completion**

K–L/1   Activities
K–L/2   Actions
K–L/3   Stage summary
K–L/4   Watchpoints
K–L/5   Action checks

Supplement
K–L/S1   Keeping the client informed
K–L/S2   Site meetings
K–L/S3   Site inspections
K–L/S4   Issuing instructions
K–L/S5   Dealing with claims
K–L/S6   Issuing certificates
K–L/S7   Preparing for handover
K–L/S8   Post-completion

255   **M**   **Feedback**

M/1   Activities
M/2   Actions
M/3   Stage summary
M/4   Watchpoints
M/5   Action checks

Supplement
M/S1   Keeping office records
M/S2   In-house appraisal
M/S3   Debriefing
M/S4   Full feedback study

269   **References and further reading**

List of Figures

Published forms and certificates	J.06	Specimen form: Clerk of Works Project Report	*Page* 202
	KL.04	Specimen form: Architect's Instruction	234
	KL.10	Specimen form: Interim Certificate and Direction	243
	KL.11	Specimen form: Certificate of Practical Completion	244
	KL.13	Specimen form: Final Certificate	246

Specimen record forms, agenda etc	PRE.01	A specimen value assessment sheet for client	14
	PRE.02	Specimen project resource planning sheet	19
	AB.04	Specimen agenda for initial design team meeting	58
	AB.05	Visits to sites and unoccupied buildings: RIBA safety code	63
	C.01	Specimen cost plan/budget estimate	81
	C.02	Specimen schedule of activities/spaces/rooms	89
	D.02	Specimen room data notes sheet	97
	E.04	Checklist of necessary drawn information	124
	E.05	Specimen registers of drawings and prints	125
	E.06	Specimen schedule of drawings required	126
	E.07	Specimen architect's drawing issue sheet	127
	E.08	Specimen design change notice and record	128
	J.07	Specimen agenda for initial project team meeting	208
	J.08	Schedule of insurance responsibilities under JCT standard forms	210
	KL.01	Specimen financial report to client	227
	KL.02	Specimen agenda for architect's site progress meeting	229
	KL.03	Specimen report form for predictive site visits	231
	KL.05	Specimen record form of architect's instructions issued	235
	KL.06	Specimen record form of site delays observed	238
	KL.07	Specimen record form of defective work	239
	KL.08	Specimen record form of claims by contractor	240
	KL.12	Specimen record form of defects reported after practical completion	245
	KL.14	Contents for a client's maintenance handbook	252

Specimen letters	AB.01	Specimen letter to architect formerly engaged on project	38
	AB.02	Specimen letter of acceptance or appointment	39
	AB.03	Specimen letter confirming preliminary agreement	40
	H.01	Specimen letter of preliminary invitation to tender	167
	H.02	Specimen letter of invitation to tender for domestic subcontract works	168
	H.03	Specimen letter to unsuccessful tenderers for specialist subcontract works or supply items	169
	H.04	Specimen letter notifying tendered prices for specialist subcontract works or supply items	169
	H.05	Specimen advance order to named subcontractor	170
	H.06	Specimen advance order to nominated subcontractor	170
	H.07	Specimen letter of preliminary invitation to tender for main contract works	173
	H.08	Specimen letter of invitation to tender for main contract works using bills of quantities, enclosing specimen form of tender	174
	H.09	Specimen letter of invitation to tender for main contract works using drawings and specifications/schedules, enclosing specimen form of tender	176
	H.10	Specimen certificate of non-collusion	178
	H.11	Specimen letter to contractor submitting most acceptable tender	179
	H.12	Specimen letter to contractor submitting second most acceptable tender	179
	H.13	Specimen letter to other unsuccessful tenderers	179
	J.01	Specimen letter to contractor notifying early start to the main contract works	197
	J.02	Specimen letter notifying unsuccessful contractors	198
	J.03	Specimen covering letter to contractor with contract documents for signature	199
	J.04	Specimen covering letter to employer with contract documents for signature	200
	J.05	Specimen letter to newly appointed clerk of works	201
	KL.09	Specimen letter in reply to a contractor's unsubstantiated claim	241

Diagrams	D.01	The process of brief and design development	94
	E.01	Design information flow: traditional procurement	119
	E.02	Design information flow: design and build procurement	120
	E.03	Design information flow: management procurement	122

Pre-Agreement

PRE/1   **Professional services**

PRE/2   **Actions**

PRE/3   **Watchpoints**

PRE/4   **Action checks**

Supplement

PRE/S1   Practice statement

PRE/S2   Selection of an architect

PRE/S3   Appointment of architect as lead consultant

PRE/S4   Appointment of architect as consultant in design and build

PRE/S5   Appointment of architect as project manager

PRE/S6   Appointment of architect as construction manager

PRE/S7   Appointment of architect as Planning Supervisor

Professional services provided by the architect can vary considerably both in nature and extent. They could be full or partial services in connection with a building project which follows the traditional pattern of the RIBA Plan of Work. They will vary according to the capacity in which the architect is engaged to act. They might be affected by the management structure set up for the project, and by the procurement method adopted. Professional services will not always be directly related to a building project.

Although there are many variables, some principles and good practice procedures will always be applicable, and it is these which form the substance of the Sixth Edition of the *Architect's Job Book*.

However, before job procedures can be considered, the job or commission itself has to be secured. This could be as a result of a direct approach made to a potential client or an invitation to discuss and negotiate or to bid in competition. This might concern only the architect or it might call for a joint submission with other professionals or partners from commerce and industry. Terms and conditions attached to an appointment are often matters for negotiation, and a careful assessment of resources required will be crucial to make realistic costings and establish viability.

It is a fact of professional life in the mid-1990s that some architects are willing to undertake a limited amount of preliminary work for a client on a no-fee basis – presumably in the hope of securing a worthwhile commission in the future. Leaving aside the wider ethical issue, any such consideration of a loss-leader is ultimately a matter for careful professional judgement and evaluation.

Where securing a commission is subject to competitive tendering, it is essential to know what criteria the client intends to apply when evaluating tenders, and what procedures will govern the submission. See Fig PRE.01 for a typical example of the kind of value assessment a client might adopt.

A successful job usually owes much to a good working relationship between the architect, other consultants, the contractor, and in particular the client. In this latter context the existence from the outset of a document which fully and clearly sets out the services, costs and procedures agreed will minimise the potential for misunderstandings and disputes arising later. It is at the Pre-Agreement Stage that arrangements for proper contractual relationships should be fully considered.

Fig PRE.01   **A specimen value assessment sheet for client**

Item	Criterion		Client weighting %	Marks awarded (out of 100)	Weighted marks
1 Technical	·1	Technical proficiency	_____	_____	_____
	·2	Innovation	_____	_____	_____
	·3	Design skills	_____	_____	_____
	·4	Relevant experience	_____	_____	_____
2 Management	·1	Quality management systems in place	_____	_____	_____
	·2	Ability to work successfully with clients to realise their objectives for the project	_____	_____	_____
	·3	Ability to work to programme	_____	_____	_____
	·4	Ability to work to budget	_____	_____	_____
	·5	Ability to work with other consultants and coordinate their work in the design	_____	_____	_____
3 Method	·1	Proposals for undertaking the work	_____	_____	_____
4 Staffing	·1	Skills of the staff who will be working on the project, if known	_____	_____	_____
5 Location			_____	_____	_____
6 Facilities	·1	Availability of relevant facilities, such as computer aided design	_____	_____	_____
Total			_____	_____	_____

Technical and management ability may be judged by relevant experience on similar projects and the level of understanding displayed by the shortlisted architects of the particular skills and approach required. This may be established through a combination of the following:

- examination of practice brochures;
- taking up references;
- examination of short written documents submitted with tenders;
- interviewing the shortlisted architects and/or asking them to make a presentation.

These could be relevant before the appointment of an architect, whether for full or partial services, under any Plan of Work stage or part of a stage, and are generally applicable regardless of procurement method.

Concerning the client

- Consider the approach made by a prospective client. If it is of interest, respond asking for further particulars.

- Arrange a preliminary meeting if appropriate to discuss requirements.

- Note the status of the prospective client. Whether an individual acting in a private capacity or representing a charitable organisation, consortium or a company etc. If a representative, then acting under what authority and with what power.

- Check whether the project is for direct occupation by the client or more in the nature of a speculative venture. Enquire about the possible involvement of a user client which might expect to be consulted.

- Make discreet enquiries about the prospective client's business record, and apparent financial position. Whether there is any known tendency to questionable business dealings or hasty resort to threats of legal action.

If in competition

- Make sure that if involved in competitive fee bidding, it is on fair and equitable terms, and that the given information is sufficient to permit preparation of a realistic bid. Confirm in writing any reservations or requests for further information.

- Agree a common policy between fellow consultants if the fee bid is to be a team effort. Agree compatible working methods, procedures, and information format.

- Consider the minimum and maximum level of services which might be appropriate for the project, but in order to remain competitive keep strictly within the stated requirements when compiling the bid. Place the bid in accordance with the tender conditions, in the form required, and accompanied by the supporting documents stipulated.

Conditions of appointment

- Identify the likely role for the architect in the project. Whether as the lead consultant; as design team leader; as a design team member; as consultant to the Employer Client in design and build; as provider of information to the Contractor Client in design and build, or even as coordinator or manager for separate trades contracts. Make an appraisal and consider carefully the implications.

- Study the terms and conditions thought at this time likely to apply to the appointment. Consider whether they follow normal practice or whether there is specially drafted wording which shows considerable client bias.

- Identify client terms which need to be checked with a construction lawyer and insurers. Be wary of conditions which might imply a level of services beyond what can be reasonably provided for the fee.

· Check what the client has asked for concerning indemnities, third party warranties, liability period, levels of professional indemnity cover etc and consider whether these are reasonable or acceptable. If being considered for the commission depends on evidence of PII cover well in excess of that presently arranged, discuss with insurers the possibility of providing such cover as an interim measure, with the certainty of extending it if and when the commission is secured.

**The Code of
Professional Conduct**

Note relevant RIBA Code of Professional Conduct requirements such as:

· The professional services to be provided must be defined beyond reasonable doubt before any agreement is entered into (Rule 1.1).

· Business interests likely to raise doubts about the integrity of an architect in the context of a particular commission must be declared (Rule 2.1).

· Enquiries should be made about whether another architect has been engaged on the project by the same client. If so, the other architect should be notified (Rule 3.5).

· Clients' money handled on their behalf by an architect should be kept in a separate identifiable account (Rule 2.10).

· Where acting as contract administrator in traditional circumstances, the Code requires the architect to be fair and impartial (Rule 1.4).

Note also relevant RIBA Code of Professional Conduct restrictions such as:

· Subletting of professional services must have the prior agreement of the client. This will also apply to situations where design is undertaken by consultants and nominated specialists (Rule 1.3).

· Simultaneous practice as an independent consultant, and a developer or a contractor, is prohibited unless it can be demonstrated that this would not compromise Code obligations (Rule 2.2).

· Acting as contract administrator while also acting directly for the contractor is prohibited (Rule 2.3).

Making a decision

· Review the scale and nature of the prospective commission, consider the benefits that might accrue and weigh these against foreseeable difficulties and assessed risks.

· Review office resources generally and decide whether it is realistic to undertake the commission with confidence that the timetable, quality of services and the budget can be met.

· Decide whether to proceed with the preparation of a competitive fee bid with or without design ideas.

· Decide whether to accept the commission if offered and put confirmation into writing.

* Take care when offering professional advice gratuitously to friends and acquaintances. The duty of care that you owe is not related to the size of fee. Even if there is no fee, you might still have a duty in tort.

* Under certain circumstances informal dealings can be construed as giving rise to contractual relationships. A contractual duty, if breached, could result in loss and an ensuing claim. Do not be casual in your dealings and inadvertently let yourself in for more than you intended.

* In the case of a commercial or industrial client, make certain precisely where the ultimate authority resides. For example, the client's company might exist within a parent body. If the company fails and is unable to pay your fees, the benefits of your work could still be available to the parent body, which might have no legal obligation for the unpaid fees.

* Where the client is a couple (married or unmarried), or a group of individuals who have formed some kind of association, be sure that you know who has authority to make decisions, give instructions and sign cheques.

* When acting for contractor clients in design and build, establish who carries the liability for design and to what extent. The contractor might not be insured against failures of design, and the liability might extend beyond the normal professional duty to exercise reasonable skill and care.

* When acting for employer clients in design and build, be wary if asked to check the Contractor's Proposals against the Employer's Requirements, and avoid 'approving' drawings submitted by contractor or subcontractors.

* When setting out in writing the professional services you agree to carry out, make absolutely clear what is *not* included. Leave no room for misunderstandings, particularly when dealing with new or inexperienced clients.

* Keep adequate and appropriate records of all dealings connected with the project. Never sacrifice proper paperwork for the sake of assumed goodwill. File everything systematically so that items can be easily found and retrieved. Never rely completely on material held on computer: it is essential to have fail-safe back-up arrangements to protect both work in progress and records which may be needed for future reference.

* Take the time and trouble to explain fully to a client what you are proposing and why. For example, statutory obligations and necessary consents, production information, procedures for appointing contractor and subcontractors may well seem daunting to the uninitiated. It is also sometimes wise to spell out the obvious – for example, that there is no such thing as a maintenance-free building and that regular and adequate maintenance is assumed when designing.

* Pick up any ambiguities or unrealistic demands in the client's requirements. Remember that a failure to warn could leave you open to allegations of negligence.

*   Assess what resources the project might require before you quote a fee.
Can you foresee problems at this stage? What are the risks, and can they be
traded off against likely benefits to the practice if the commission is won?
Fig PRE.02 is a project resource planning sheet. Whether prepared manually
or as a spreadsheet this could provide essential information for a fee bid,
and be a tool for monitoring small jobs.

*   Be realistic when negotiating. Price for the client's stated requirements at
the outset, no more and no less. You will need to be competitive, but if you
quote a fee that is unrealistically low it might mean that you have to cut
corners and the quality of service you are able to provide will suffer
accordingly. There are obvious risks in putting yourself under this kind of
pressure.

*   A successful negotiator knows how far to go and when to stop. The aim
should never be to secure a commission at any price.

*   Never assume that the commission is won until you have received written
confirmation of acceptance.

Fig PRE.02   **Specimen project resource planning sheet**

Job no: Job title:

Project resource planning sheet

Budget cost _____ Commencement _____ Completion _____

Estimated number of site visits _____

Stage		A–B	C	D	E	F–G	H	J	K–L	
Start										
Finish										
STAFF grade/name	£ per hr	Hours	Hours	Hours	Hours	Hours	Hours	Hours	Hours	Total £
Ivor Barch – partner	100	10	5							1,500
C. Smith – job architect	75	10	25	40	40	40			25	13,500
W. Bloggs – technician	25	2	10	10	120	200				8,550
Stage Total										
EXPENSES										

1. Estimate duration of Work Stages with start and finish entries.
2. List staff assigned to job, grade, unit rate and estimated hours under Work Stages. Rates should include for overheads, profit and reserves.
3. Enter estimated expenses likely to be incurred against headings such as car mileage, travel fares, subsistence, etc.

| Total | | | | | | | | | | |

		Tick if relevant	Initial if completed
01	Prepare and activate strategy to target potential clients		
02	Respond at once to approaches from potential clients		
03	Identify nature of commission and intended role for architect		
04	Identify nature of project and professional services needed		
05	Check soundness of client's business dealings		
06	Identify status and authority of any client representative		
07	Check whether project is for client's own occupation		
08	Check details of any user client or interested third party		
09	Arrange personal meeting with client to establish rapport		
10	Consider likely benefits of project and assess risks		
11	If in competition, check it is on a fair basis		
12	If initiating a team bid, agree procedures and terms at outset		
13	If part of a team bid, check procedures and terms at outset		
14	If about to bid, check procedures etc required for submission		
15	Check there is no conflict with professional Code, rules		
16	Check client requirement for PI insurance, warranties etc		
17	Check with insurers if PI cover is inadequate for bid		
18	Take expert advice if client seeks to impose onerous conditions		
19	Check office resources wrt services, timetable, fee		
20	Decide whether to bid/accept or decline commission		
21	Prepare appropriate submission/response		
22			
23			
24			
25			
26			
27			
28			
29			
30			

Supplement

PRE/S1   **Practice statement**

PRE/S2   **Selection of an architect**

PRE/S3   **Appointment of architect as lead consultant**

PRE/S4   **Appointment of architect as consultant in design and build**

PRE/S5   **Appointment of architect as project manager**

PRE/S6   **Appointment of architect as construction manager**

PRE/S7   **Appointment of architect as Planning Supervisor**

Architects intending to approach, or being approached by new clients need to have information about their practice ready to hand. General information might be immediately accessible from a practice brochure, or from entries in the RIBA Practice Index or the Directory of Practices. Detailed information required in the context of a particular project might need to be specially assembled. Some client bodies require this in a specific format, but nearly all will expect information to be included about the following.

- Practice name and style, addresses, telephone, fax.
- Status of practice: whether sole principal, partnership, company etc.
- Directors or partners: names, photos, brief cvs.
- Building type experience relevant to the particular enquiry.
- Specialist skills in-house or where to be obtained.
- Recent commissions: details, illustrations, contact names.
- Practice computer systems.
- Overseas experience and completed commissions, if relevant.
- Languages in which the practice is fluent, if relevant.
- Practice quality management systems, QA status.
- Consultants with whom the practice normally collaborates.
- Team being offered for the particular commission, with brief cvs.
- Professional indemnity cover arrangements (but check with insurers before divulging information).

The appointment of an architect may be handled directly by the client or indirectly through a project manager acting on his behalf. It could be for the full traditional services where the architect is lead consultant or for a limited appointment where the architect might be engaged to lead the design team, or simply to take on a design concept role. Regardless of the nature of the appointment or the procurement method adopted, the selection of an architect is likely to follow one of the following recognised procedures.

One to one negotiation

The architect is chosen on the basis of personal contact or recommendation, perhaps after a series of interviews. This procedure has the following features:
. Suitable for any project.
· Particularly suitable where services required are not yet formulated or the initial brief is still unclear.
· The client can have the opportunity of professional help in preparing an initial brief.
· Negotiations over services, terms and fees can be carried out using a standard schedule of services as a focus for discussion.

Competitive interview

The architect is chosen primarily on the basis of a presentation to some stipulated form. The main features with this procedure include:
· Suitable for projects of any size.
· A limited number of architects may be shortlisted to make presentations.
· The architect can expect the client to supply a broad outline of the project and to state exactly what the presentation should cover.
· The presentation can be in written form only, or involve an interview, as stipulated by the client in the invitation. Any design content can be a matter for the architect, but will not normally extend beyond broad concepts.
· After the presentation, the preferred firm can negotiate services and fees etc.

Qualifications-based selection

The architect is chosen primarily on the basis of quality, by which is meant technical qualifications, design and performance potential and general suitability for the project in question. This approach to selection is widely and successfully used in the USA for public sector procurement following the introduction of 'The Brooks Act' in 1972, and there are currently moves to promote the adoption of Brooks Act selection procedures in the UK for both private and public sector work.

After appropriate advertisement an initial list of firms is compiled from which no more than three are invited for interview and discussion. There is no mention of fees until the preferred firm is selected. If it proves impossible to agree a 'fair and reasonable' fee, negotiations with that firm are irrevocably terminated and fresh negotiations begin with the next preferred firm.

The Brooks approach has the undeniable merit of placing quality before any other consideration and, in the US at any rate, is perceived to be best value for taxpayers' money in the long term. Variants of the method, where for example there is an initial 'balancing' of price and quality, are also being suggested as more satisfactory approaches for an emerging band of farsighted and enlightened clients.

**Fee tender
(without design)**

The architect is chosen solely on the basis of the fee quoted, that is, the procedure is geared to the competitiveness of the fee.
- Unlikely to be suitable for more complex projects, and those under £500,000 capital value.
- A limited number of firms (say 5 or 6) who accept invitations are sent tender documents. All must receive identical information.
- The architect can expect the client to state precisely which services are required and to provide an initial brief for the project.
- Clients may stipulate that the fee quotation is accompanied by a resources schedule or other specified information.
- After receipt of satisfactory tenders, the client can be expected to enter into an agreement. There is little scope for negotiation, and the RIBA Code of Professional Conduct prohibits revising a fee quotation to take account of the fee quoted by another architect for the same service.

**Fee tender
(without design)
using the
Two Envelope System**

The architect is chosen both on the basis of technical qualifications and on a fee quoted. Each is considered separately.
- Unlikely to be suitable for projects of less than £500,000 capital value.
- A limited number of firms (say 5 or 6) who accept invitations are sent tender documents. All must receive identical information.
- The architect can expect the client to state precisely which services are required and to provide a schedule of accommodation and full design criteria.
- The architect should expect the client to state the criteria to be used when evaluating the tenders.
- Two envelopes will normally be provided for tender submissions, clearly marked:
(1) 'Qualifications' (the technical submission).
(2) 'Fee' (the tender and quoted figure in a form stipulated by the client).

The Qualifications envelopes are opened first and the firms placed in order of preference. Then the Fee envelope from the preferred tenderer (only) is opened. Negotiation might subsequently be needed to arrive at a fair and reasonable figure, but Rule 3.3 of the RIBA Code of Professional Conduct must be observed. Only in the event of failure to reach a satisfactory outcome should the Fee envelope of the next preferred tenderer be opened.

**Design submission
with fee proposal**

The architect is chosen both on the basis of a design submission and on a fee quoted. Each is considered separately under the Two Envelope System.
- Suitable for larger projects (eg over £1 million).
- A limited number of firms (say three) who accept invitations are sent tender documents. All must receive full identical information.
- Clients should expect to pay a fee to all tenderers who submit detailed design ideas, and this will usually restrict the number of invitations. Architects taking part in such an arrangement would be wise to secure a formal agreement with the client to this effect.
- Architects can expect the client to state precisely the nature and extent of services required, and provide adequate design criteria for the project.
- Two envelopes will normally be provided for tender submissions, clearly marked:
(1) 'Design Proposals'.
(2) 'Fee Tender'.

The Design Proposals envelopes from each of the tenderers is opened first and the firms placed in order of preference. Then the Fee envelope from the preferred tenderer (only) is opened. Negotiation might subsequently be needed to arrive at a fair and reasonable figure, but Rule 3.3 of the RIBA Code of Professional Conduct must be observed.

Design ideas competition

The architect is chosen solely on the basis of design ideas. The procedure does not involve fee tenders, for the fee is stated in the competition conditions.

- Suitable, in theory, for important projects regardless of size. In practice, application is likely to be restricted by the relative high cost to both client and architect.
- The architect can expect the client to provide a project brief, to define the professional services required, and to appoint a panel of assessors. This requires a professional input on the part of the client.
- Competition may be restricted to invited participants, and architects taking part in such an arrangement can expect to be paid a fee. A formal agreement with the client to that effect is advisable.
- Competition may be open, but there is obviously a high cost risk for architects who participate.
- Competitions are best run to procedures fully set out in *Architectural Competitions*, an RIBA code of practice. Rule 3.7 of the RIBA Code of Professional Conduct prohibits architects from entering competitions which the RIBA has declared to be unacceptable.

Guidance on architects' fees may be found in *Engaging an Architect: Guidance for Clients on Fees*, published by the RIBA in 1994.

Note: Contracts for professional services may also be subject to The Public Services Contracts Regulations 1993 (SI 1993 No. 3228). Regulation 3 defines what is a 'contracting authority', and Regulation 21 sets out the criteria for awarding a contract. Regulation 24 is concerned with design contests. The Regulations only apply to services which are likely to be above a certain threshold, which at the time of writing is 200,000 ECUs.

Information needed by architects before tendering

When responding to an initial enquiry

Architects invited to join a tender list will need certain information before considering their response. The client should be expected to state, for example:
- the number of architects approached;
- the nature and scale of the project;
- the location of the proposed works;
- the client's budget figure;
- the anticipated time-scale;
- the nature and scope of the professional services;
- how the fee is to be expressed;
- procedures to be followed for the submission;
- criteria to be used when making a value assessment of submissions;
- closing time, date, and where submissions are to be sent, and period during which tender is to remain open for acceptance.

When making a Fee plus Technical Submission

Information all as listed above, together with additional relevant information, such as:
- funding arrangements for the project;
- client's working practices or other constraints which should be taken into account;
- schedule of accommodation requirements;
- procurement method preferred;
- type of contract envisaged;
- information concerning site or existing structures;
- other consultants/specialists already appointed or to be appointed.

When making a Fee plus Design Ideas Submission

Information all as listed above, together with additional relevant information, such as:
- detailed schedule of accommodation needs;
- critical functional relationships of spaces or plan elements;
- environmental performance standards required;
- level of quality specifications to be satisfied;
- known statutory controls and details of any agreements already reached concerning planning or environmental matters.

In the traditional or conventional appointment the architect is leader of the design team and as such is responsible for coordinating and integrating the work of other consultants and specialists. If lead consultant the architect is also responsible for the production information programme and tender action, with or without the assistance of a quantity surveyor. General inspection of progress and quality of the work under construction, and administering the terms of the building contract are also traditional functions.

On many projects, particularly those of a smaller scale where the client wishes to engage only one professional consultant, this arrangement will still apply. On larger projects, the architect's commission is increasingly being confined to certain Plan of Work stages, or designated activities not necessarily to a Plan of Work format. Sometimes the appointment will be for full services, but moving stage by stage. With arrangements where a more flexible approach to appointment is necessary, particular care is needed.

Typical duties

Typical duties of an architect undertaking services specific to building projects might include:
- consulting the client about the proposed work;
- informing the client of duties under the CDM Regulations;
- investigating the feasibility of the requirements, and reporting;
- advising the client about any limitations on the use of land or buildings;
- preparing outline proposals, a scheme design, detail design drawings etc;
- advising on the need for statutory and other consents, and preparing sufficient information for applications to be made;
- preparing sufficient production information for consultants and specialists to develop their proposals, coordinating these and integrating them into the overall scheme;
- bringing contract documentation to a final state for inviting tenders, and advising on tendering and the appointment of the main contractor;
- administering the terms of the building contract and inspecting as relevant the performance of the contractor;
- issuing further reasonably necessary information, issuing empowered instructions, and acting as certifier as the contract requires, including issue of the final certificate;
- arranging for the preparation of record information and manuals.

A standard appointing document should preferably be used, but this should never be sent 'cold' to a client. It should first form a focus for discussion on the professional services which need to be commissioned, and only then be completed as a formal confirmation of what has been agreed.

If a preliminary appointment is needed pending formal agreement about the full services to be provided, a letter can be used incorporating the appropriate references. A letter activating appointment for specific stages can often be used in conjunction with a formal appointing document. A variation in services already formally agreed, or additional services to be provided, can often be imported by a letter supplementing the original document. It is important to be meticulous over such matters however, and to take legal advice where appropriate.

Appointment of architect as consultant in design and build

A majority of design and build contracts, with the possible exception of package deals, involve an architect. This is a role quite different from that with the traditional commission, in that the architect acts solely as consultant to either an Employer Client or a Contractor Client at any one time. It is not uncommon for the architect to be engaged by both, but this would be sequential, never simultaneous, and would entail either the so-called consultant switch or novation. Even under this kind of arrangement it is often extremely difficult to separate clearly legal accountability and design responsibility. The degree of involvement with either Employer or Contractor will vary enormously depending on the particular arrangements. An architect has no stated function in connection with the building contract.

Typical duties – Employer Client

Typical duties of an architect appointed as consultant to an Employer Client might include:
- advising on the initial brief;
- informing the Employer Client of duties under the CDM Regulations;
- carrying out a site appraisal;
- advising on the appointment of other consultants;
- advising on and taking part in discussions with statutory and other bodies;
- preparing outline proposals and making application for outline planning permission;
- advising on development of the brief for the Employer's Requirements;
- developing design concept drawings as appropriate for the Employer's Requirements;
- advising on tendering procedures;
- advising on contract matters;
- examining the Contractor's Proposals, including design and the contract sum analysis, and offering advice;
- acting as Employer's Agent under the contract during the construction of the works;
- visiting the site during construction and reporting back to the Employer Client;
- advising the Employer Client on his obligations under the contract, and assisting in the drafting of statements;
- inspecting the works on behalf of the client prior to practical completion and advising the Employer Client;
- checking the contractor's as built drawings and operating/maintenance manuals;
- advising the Employer Client on the Employer's Final Account and Employer's Final Statement as appropriate.

Typical duties – Contractor Client

Typical duties of an architect appointed as consultant to a Contractor Client might include:
- examining the Employer's Requirements and all available information, and discussing a strategy for tendering;
- visiting the site, and noting all relevant constraints;
- checking arrangements for compliance with the CDM Regulations;
- advising on the appointment of other consultants;
- checking with authorities on statutory consents obtained and required;
- advising on the need for specialist subcontractors;
- fulfilling the role of design team leader;
- providing the Contractor Client with sketches, specification notes etc for initial tendering purposes;

- advising about limitations or inconsistencies in the Employer's Requirements;
- providing the Contractor Client with drawings, specifications, samples etc to support the Contractor's Proposals;
- after the contract has been awarded, developing and amending drawings and other documents in the Contractor's Proposals for contract documentation;
- developing design details;
- applying for statutory and other necessary approvals;
- preparing performance specifications and other detailed information for subcontractor tendering;
- preparing production information drawings, details, schedules, specification notes for the Contractor Client;
- inspecting work during construction and reporting to the Contractor Client;
- preparing additional drawings etc as necessary for submission to the Employer in the event of change orders;
- visiting manufacturers' workshops/factories as necessary and reporting to the Contractor Client;
- assisting in the preparation of as built drawings, operating/maintenance manuals etc;
- inspecting the works prior to practical completion and advising the Contractor Client.

The appointment of an architect in these situations is best secured by using the standard appointing documents specific to design and build, ie an Employer Client version or a Contractor Client version. In the event that the architect has a continuing professional involvement by way of either the consultant switch or novation, both versions may be needed together with a specially drafted Tripartite Agreement. This arrangement usually calls for careful handling, specialist legal advice, and expert drafting.

Appointment of architect
as project manager

The project manager is the individual or firm primarily employed to look after the client's interests throughout the stages of a project in collaboration with the design team, including the cost consultant. The project manager's remit can be very wide, ranging initially from managing the brief through to managing the marketing or disposal of the completed project.

The project manager is usually responsible for the overall direction of the design team, other consultants and specialists, contractor and subcontractors. Administering the contract might be undertaken by the project manager or by a contract administrator working in close collaboration. The project manager's duties will vary considerably according to the nature of the project and the wording of the contract. The appointment of a project manager might be appropriate in traditional procurement, design and build, or for a management contract.

Typical duties

Typical duties of an independent project manager might include:
- assisting in the preparation and development of the brief;
- informing the client of duties under the CDM Regulations;
- arranging for feasibility studies and reports;
- arranging for measures required by health and safety legislation;
- preparing the project management structure and plan;
- advising on the procurement method;
- arranging the appointment of consultants and specialists;
- checking professional indemnity insurances, warranties etc;
- instructing consultants on feasibility studies, research, surveys;
- coordinating the design process;
- preparing and maintaining an overall cost plan;
- organising communication and information systems;
- arranging consultations/negotiations with statutory bodies;
- arranging monthly reports to the client on cost and completion forecasts;
- monitoring the performance etc of the design team and consultants;
- arranging tender documentation;
- organising pre-qualification checks on contractors;
- evaluating tenders and preparing recommendations;
- participating in the selection and appointment of the contractor;
- arranging for the appointment of a construction supervisor/client's agent;
- assembling contract documentation;
- arranging for the appointment of an adjudicator and services as required;
- issuing instructions and variation orders;
- issuing extensions of time notices;
- preparing valuations and monitoring the budget;
- arranging commissioning and witness tests;
- developing a maintenance programme and staff training;
- organising handover/occupation procedures;
- issuing the practical completion certificate, preparing the final account;
- organising maintenance manuals and as built information;
- planning facilities management;
- advising on the marketing/disposal of the project;
- checking that defects are remedied, issuing the final certificate.

The role of project manager, for which some architects might well have the skills and aptitude, should be seen as separate and distinct from the architect's traditional role. It should not be confused with what many architects think of simply as managing the project. Architects accepting an appointment as project manager will need a suitably drafted document; RIBA standard forms for the appointment of an architect will not be appropriate.

The construction manager is the individual or organisation employed primarily to manage the construction stages of the project in collaboration with the design team, including the cost consultant. The appointee will be a specialist with contracting experience, paid by fee, and should preferably be appointed early (at the same time as the design team) so that he can participate in initial discussions. However, in practice the construction manager is often not brought in until the pre-construction stages are well advanced. Construction of the project is carried out by trades contractors, each having a direct contract with the employer but working under the direction of the construction manager.

A construction manager will be appropriate only where there are separate trades contracts which need to be coordinated.

Services which can be provided by a construction manager are held by some people to include helping to establish the client's requirements at pre-construction stages. A construction manager may certainly make a positive contribution at project design stage, but duties will vary considerably according to the nature of the project, the timing of the appointment and the wording of the contract.

Typical duties

Typical duties of a construction manager might include:
- arranging for meetings at design stages between client, design team and proposed trades contractors who will have a design responsibility;
- recommending the most economical materials and methods to meet the requirements of specification and sound construction practice;
- commenting on project drawings and project specification as appropriate, and advising on production information for issue by trades contractors;
- advising the design team on the division of the project into trades contracts;
- advising on the need for works at pre-construction stages, eg exploratory, mock-ups, tests of particular components etc;
- arranging as appropriate for checks of the outline cost plan, the preparation of a project cost plan and cash flow forecasts;
- advising on measures necessary to satisfy statutory obligations, liaising with local and statutory authorities about construction and on site matters, and monitoring compliance by trades contractors;
- preparing a project programme showing lead times for trades contracts;
- preparing detailed week by week programmes, expanding and updating these during the progress of the works;
- advising the client on insurances to be taken out in respect of the project;
- preparing a schedule of tender events showing earliest start and anticipated finishing dates for all trades contracts;
- preparing, in consultation with the design team, a suitable tender list of trades contractors, checking references and resource capability;
- advising on tender procedures and participating in interviews, together with the client and design team as appropriate;
- evaluating tenders and preparing recommendations;
- advising the client on materials or plant to be ordered prior to placing trades contracts;
- arranging for adequate information for setting out, and coordinating this as necessary;
- issuing empowered instructions to trades contractors;
- receiving, reviewing and coordinating information, shop drawings etc from trades contractors in consultation with the design team;
- providing management, administration and planning of trades contracts operations; monitoring methods, progress and quality;
- coordinating trades contracts operations in line with the project plan;

Typical duties
continued

- arranging regular meetings with trades contractors to monitor progress and ascertain information requirements; chairing regular site meetings, issuing minutes and providing the client with monthly reports;
- preparing valuations and dealing with applications for payment from trades contractors;
- preparing interim and final accounts for each trade contractor;
- issuing certificates as required by the contract, including practical completion, in consultation with the design team;
- arranging for commissioning and testing;
- checking that defects are remedied;
- obtaining from each trade contractor relevant records, as built drawings and operating/maintenance manuals.

Acting in the role of the construction manager is unlikely to interest the majority of architects directly, who will only rarely have the necessary experience, skills and aptitude – at least as far as projects of any size are concerned. Architects involved in this kind of procurement method are more likely to be acting as designer or design team leader under the direction of the construction manager.

However, architects sometimes find themselves handling smaller projects where there is no main contractor and the work is carried out by direct labour, sometimes volunteers, or through a series of separate trades contracts. If asked to organise such operations they might be acting as the construction manager with all the attendant responsibilities for setting up the site, programming and coordination. This situation is not covered by standard appointing documents, and it would be well to check with insurers before undertaking to provide this kind of consultancy service. An appropriately drafted agreement would be needed.

Under The Construction (Design and Management) Regulations 1994 the client In most jobs will be under a statutory duty to appoint a Planning Supervisor and a Principal Contractor.

Architects might wish to consider appointment as a Planning Supervisor either on a job where they are also acting as the architect or one where architectural services are provided by others. In all cases an appointment as Planning Supervisor should be seen as distinct from the provision of architectural services and the RIBA publishes a suitable Form of Appointment PS/95.

The Planning Supervisor will need a sound knowledge of design and construction processes and practice, and of health and safety matters relevant to the particular project. The appointment is to be made as soon as is practicable after the client has sufficient information about the project to be able to assess the appointee's competence and adequacy of resources for health and safety.

Typical duties

Typical duties of an independent Planning Supervisor might include:
- informing the client of duties under the CDM Regulations;
- advising the client on the competence and resources of designers as relevant to health and safety obligations;
- issuing statutory notices to the Health and Safety Executive;
- ensuring so far as reasonably possible that potential hazards are identified, eliminated or reduced at design stages;
- ensuring that all design team members and others contributing to the design (eg specialists/subcontractors) cooperate over health and safety obligations;
- ensuring that a pre-tender Health and Safety Plan is ready for inclusion with tender information;
- attending pre-tender meetings with invited Principal Contractors to check adequacy of resources for health and safety obligations, and written health and safety policy statements;
- advising the client on the competence and resources of contractors relevant to health and safety obligations;
- checking that the Principal Contractor is provided with reasonably necessary health and safety information before construction commences;
- appraising the Principal Contractor's construction phase Health and Safety Plan and advising the client;
- monitoring the Principal Contractor's development of or changes to the Health and Safety Plan following variations or additional work, and advising the client as necessary;
- observing the Principal Contractor's compliance with the Health and Safety Plan during construction of the works, and advising the client if there are departures;
- obtaining necessary information for the Health and Safety File during the design and construction stages;
- preparing the Health and Safety File and advising the client on its safe keeping and future use.

The role of Planning Supervisor is one which on major projects might be undertaken by an independently appointed architect who has undergone the necessary training. On simpler projects the architect as lead consultant might be well placed to take on the additional but separate role of Planning Supervisor. However, this is a relatively new statutory appointment and the services to be provided need to be fully and precisely indicated. Any architect accepting such an appointment will need to understand fully the implications, be properly trained, and have appropriate indemnity cover. It is a function which could attract considerable liability in the event of injury to persons, or losses to clients should the works be delayed because of incidents or intervention by the Health and Safety Executive.

Architects should remember that even where a minor or domestic job is not notifiable to the Health and Safety Executive and there is no Planning Supervisor, the requirements on the Designer under the CDM Regulations will still apply.

Inception and Feasibility

A–B/1   **Activities**

A–B/2   **Actions**

A–B/3   **Stage summary**

A–B/4   **Watchpoints**

A–B/5   **Action checks**

Supplement

A–B/S1   The briefing process

A–B/S2   Project brief checklist

A–B/S3   Design team appointments and working

A–B/S4   Planning permission, other consents and approvals

A–B/S5   Health and safety checklists

A–B/S6   A project quality plan

A–B/S7   Inspecting the site

A–B/S8   Financial appraisal

Description

Stage A must be present in all commissions for architects' services, whether this is at the inception of the project or after certain actions have already been taken, as for example when the architect is appointed by a project manager or acting for a Contractor Client in design and build. It is the time when requirements are clarified, a strategy for action prepared, and terms of appointment agreed.

Stage B includes such studies as may be relevant to determine what services will be necessary and whether it is feasible to achieve the project aims within the defined constraints. Such studies may be undertaken initially by a client organisation with in-house expertise, or by a project manager before the appointment of other consultants. Professional advisers may be commissioned solely for Stage B, more particularly in the case of major projects where demonstrable impartiality and objectivity is required by a client body. However, for the majority of commissions the architect as designer is well placed to undertake feasibility studies, advise on alternative design and constructional approaches, and identify what might be imposed by legislative and other constraints.

Terminology

* The RIBA Plan of Work refers separately to Stage A as Inception and Stage B as Feasibility.

* RIBA standard appointing documents generally refer to a combined Stage A–B Inception and Feasibility.

* Different terminology is sometimes used where the commission relates to work on Historic Buildings (eg Stage A–B Initial Briefing and Appraisal). With Community Architecture projects the scope of services under Stage A–B might be extended to include for example services to the User Client concerning group organisation and participation, advice on revenue funding etc.

* Design and build services, whether for Employer Client or Contractor Client, will usually refer to Stage A–B Inception and Feasibility.

General procedures

· Check whether any other architects were formerly involved with the project. If so, check that their appointment has been properly terminated and notify them in writing of your own appointment, when this has been formally concluded. Fig AB.01 is a specimen letter.

· Establish the scope and content of Stage A–B. Put it into context particularly if material produced is likely to be acted upon by others taking over subsequent stages. Procurement method could be an important consideration.

· Agree with the client the extent of professional services for Stage A–B and confirm in writing. If possible establish whether this is to be a continuing involvement for full services or likely to be a partial service confined to this Stage.

· Agree with the client the methods and levels of payment, eg whether a lump sum, percentages, rates or some other means, and confirm in writing.

· Confirm acceptance of the appointment by completing a formal Memorandum of Agreement, or perhaps in the case of small works, by sending a letter of acceptance (see Fig AB.02). Should it prove premature to enter into a formal Memorandum at this point, when for example the extent of professional involvement cannot yet be determined, then enter into a preliminary agreement as an interim measure, clearly identified as such (see Fig AB.03).

· Open project files and allocate code letter or number to the project in accordance with office practice. Check with the client the full project title to be used.

· Begin to compile a record of all key persons involved in the project together with addresses, phone and fax numbers etc. Check that names, titles or descriptions are correct and check spelling. Circulate to all concerned.

· Set up office procedures for recording time spent on the project, by whom and the rates chargeable, and for noting expenses and disbursements incurred.

Fig AB.01   **Specimen letter to architect formerly engaged on project**

We understand that you were engaged by (the clients) to work on this project but that the arrangement has been properly terminated.

Under Rule 3.5 of the RIBA Code of Professional Conduct we are obliged to notify you that (the clients) have now appointed us as architects for this project.

We would be pleased to have your written confirmation that there are no matters outstanding which should be drawn to our attention at this stage.

Fig AB.02   **Specimen letter of acceptance or appointment**

Only appropriate for straightforward situations where it is considered preferable to use a letter rather than the more formal Memorandum of Agreement. This specimen letter is based on the one included in the RIBA's Conditions of Engagement (CE/95), and the text should be carefully adapted to suit the particular circumstances.

Thank you for inviting me to act as your architect in connection with the above project. I have much pleasure in confirming my terms.

I propose that the services, the conditions of appointment and the basis of fee calculation relating to this appointment are all as described in the RIBA's Conditions of Engagement (CE/95). I enclose a copy for your retention.

The specific services which I propose are listed in the CE/95 Schedule of Services, and my fees are set out in the CE/95 Schedule of Fees and Expenses. Standard conditions of appointment are included in CE/95, and this letter of appointment, the Schedule of Fees and Expenses and the Conditions of Appointment comprise our agreement.

I take this opportunity to remind you that there will be duties under the Construction (Design and Management) Regulations 1994. I enclose the RIBA's guidance booklet for clients on the Health and Safety Regulations which you may find helpful. Guidance is also available from the Health and Safety Executive.

I will submit monthly accounts for my fees and expenses. VAT is chargeable on these. Should it become necessary to make any disbursements on your behalf, for example the fees to accompany applications for planning permission and building regulations approval, you will be charged for these at their net cost.

I do not anticipate that it will be necessary to seek further advice from consultants or specialists for this project.

I hope that these arrangements are acceptable to you. Would you please sign and return to me the enclosed copy of this letter as confirmation of our agreement.

Fig AB.03 **Specimen letter confirming preliminary agreement**

An interim measure only to be used in particular circumstances.

We are writing about the terms of our appointment for this project.

You have asked us to undertake some preliminary services so that the project may proceed, and we confirm these as follows:

....
....

It is understood that if you subsequently instruct us to undertake other preliminary services, you will confirm this in writing. All these services will be charged on a time basis at the following rates:

Principals	£ ...... per	
Senior architectural staff	£ ...... per	
Other architectural staff	£ ...... per	
Administrative staff	£ ...... per	

In addition, the following expenses will be charged:

....
....

Invoices will be submitted monthly. VAT is chargeable, where applicable, at the current standard rate on all fees and expenses.

For the above services to be provided effectively, you will also need to appoint:

....
....

You should note that other financial commitments at this stage may include:

....
....

We will provide these services on the basis of the conditions included in the Form of Agreement, a copy of which is enclosed [if appropriate at this stage].

We envisage that this preliminary appointment will continue for approximately ...... months while we conclude the principal Agreement. When the principal Agreement has been entered into, this appointment will be subsumed into it, and fees invoiced under this letter will rank as payments on account.

Please confirm your acceptance of the appointment set out in this letter by signing the enclosed copy and returning it to us.

- Assess office resources needed for Stage A–B and ensure that they are adequate and available.

- Prepare a project quality plan in an appropriate form. This will include procedures to assist control, verification and recording of actions, in accordance with guidance given for an office manual in *Quality Management*, published by the RIBA. A quality plan provides a mechanism to link the specific requirements of the project to an office quality management system which might already exist. It will not necessarily mean the development of a new document or procedures over and above those that already exist.

- Establish who is to be the design team leader and who will lead the office design unit. Identify personnel, roles, accountability and lines of communication.

- Set up procedures for checking progress against the timetable for services regularly, and for taking corrective action if needed.

- Set up procedures for checking expenditure against the office job cost allocation regularly.

- Arrange for regular reports to the client on fees and expenses incurred, and for accounts to be submitted at agreed intervals.

- Check with professional indemnity insurers if the project seems likely to call for services outside those covered by the policy. For example the architect might find it necessary to engage other consultants direct, or might be called upon to give advice on self-build operations, or might act as manager for a series of separate trades contracts. Cover could also be called into question because of the nature or scale of operations, or because of stipulations by the client as to the amount or duration of cover required.

Preliminary issues   **Concerning the client**

- Obtain from the client the project requirements, budget and timetable. Check these carefully, question incompatibilities and agree priorities. Help to formulate the Initial Brief.

- Enquire whether additional services will be wanted which are not included under the Agreement. These might extend to special studies, community surveys and participation exercises with a user client, attendance at meetings etc.

- Enquire whether the client wishes to ensure confidentiality for the project. If not, and publicity is sought, is this likely to involve wider consultation, eg presentations to a user client or local amenity bodies.

- Check that the client has made organisational arrangements to deal with questions, supply information and take decisions. Appointed representatives of the client should have the authority to act.

- Confirm the role of the architect, ie whether appointed as lead consultant, design team leader or member, or working under a project manager. Direct access to the client, particularly at design stages, is highly desirable.

Preliminary issues
continued

- Advise the client on the need to appoint a quantity surveyor and other consultants or specialists. Confirm who will make the appointments, the basis of agreements and the scope of such services.

- Explain to the client the need for various approvals under national legislation concerned with planning and building, and the additional requirements of any local legislation or legislation for the particular building type which might apply. Inform the client of fees payable to the relevant authority at the time of application.

- Inform the client of the obligations of a client under the CDM Regulations, and other health and safety legislation, as appropriate. Alert the client of the need to appoint a Planning Supervisor, where the law requires this.

- Check that the client is able to provide necessary information about the site or existing buildings, and which will need to be first verified by the client's solicitors. Such information might concern details of ownership, leases, boundaries, covenants, easements, party wall agreements and other land charges.

- Check whether the client is able to provide copies of earlier studies or proposals for the site or buildings which might prove useful.

- Check whether the client has a deposited Health and Safety File relating to the site or work carried out on the building previously. If so this must be made available.

- Explain to the client the options for procurement and note any matters which could affect the particular choice.

Concerning other bodies

- Hold preliminary discussions with the Planning Officer on such matters as:
  - availability of Statutory Development Plan, relevance of Planning Policy Guidance Notes, design notes or guides published by the particular authority;
  - special circumstances which need to be taken into account (eg Listed Building, Conservation Area, Enterprise Zone, Development Corporation etc);
  - whether an environmental impact assessment will be expected or helpful;
  - known existence of hazardous substances or conditions due to earlier uses, likelihood of archaeological remains etc.

- Enquire whether the proposed work requires planning permission, and if so which applications would be relevant.

- Discover the attitude of the Planning Officer towards the principle of development as proposed and whether serious difficulties might be expected. Establish the measure of consultation which the Planning Officer would welcome or expect.

- Check with the relevant statutory bodies whether there are plans for compulsory purchase, or land take proposals for, say, road improvements which could affect use of the site.

· Enquire about restrictions on site development potential due to mains or cables either below ground or overhead, and whether or not subject to easements or wayleaves.

· Check whether, particularly in the case of alterations to an existing building, the local authority Building Control Department might be sympathetic to dispensations under building regulations.

· Enquire about any concerns that the Fire Authority, police or military might have, particularly in an area of high sensitivity, and which might influence development or design.

· Check on the position and capacity of mains drainage and supplies from statutory undertakers.

· Enquire about possible sources of funding or grant aid if this is a relevant factor. This might take the form of assistance from government departments, statutory bodies, local authorities, English Heritage etc, or charitable trusts, and many organisations with limited funds but still useful in aggregate. Financial assistance is often subject to conditions which could affect design and specification proposals.

Team working

Check scope of professional services agreed with design team members as they are appointed. Services should be adequate for the Stage, with no overlap and without leaving areas of uncertainty.

· Confirm agreed policy of consultants and specialists concerning accountability, warranties, professional indemnity insurance etc.

· Confirm composition of design team. Identify functional relationship to Planning Supervisor and project manager (if appointed) and establish the authority of the design team leader.

· Establish patterns for communication between client, Planning Supervisor, project manager and design team leader. Procedures for design team members should be clearly set out and closely followed throughout the project.

· Appraise Initial Brief and agree input to the Stage by design team members. Check for compatibility in working methods, systems, software etc.

· Confirm means for integrating and coordinating effort and input of design team members.

· Confirm Stage timetable for services and note its relationship to the project timetable as agreed with the client. The timetable should show critical points by which information from the client and design team members will be required.

· Establish programme and pattern for design team meetings. Fig AB.04 is a specimen agenda for an initial design team meeting.

Preliminary issues
continued

Costs

- Appraise client budget figures and identify the sums included for actual construction work.

- Review client requirements, programme and budget to assess compatibility. If not in balance report to client and seek clarification on priorities.

- Prepare cost appraisal for Stage A–B and compare with original client budget figures or as last amended. Report to the client. The cost appraisal should be structured under appropriate headings, eg capital costs, costs in use, total project costs, value, viability etc. It will normally be prepared by the quantity surveyor, if appointed as yet. On small jobs where there is no QS, cost estimates may need to be prepared by the architect.

- Alert client to the possible effects on the cost of the project due to inflation, and the application of VAT.

- Advise on possible sources of funding or grant aid and, if instructed, help to prepare a case or application.

- Initiate resource control procedures for the office, and monitor expenditure against allocation of fee for the Stage.

- Report to the client on cost matters at agreed intervals.

Approvals/consents

- Check for any existing relevant permission, approval or consent still current. Obtain the original notices if possible.

- Check what legislation is likely to be relevant. Obtain access to the text of Acts, SIs and Approved Documents or Approved Codes of Practice, and study them.

- List authorities or bodies which may need to be contacted, identify particular officers, names, addresses, phone numbers etc.

- Check information obtained from planning and land registers and other legal documents which might indicate consents necessary from third parties. List persons who may need to be contacted, eg landlord, estate surveyor, lessees, adjoining owners etc.

- Hold preliminary discussions as appropriate before making formal submissions for permission, approval or consent.

- Prepare application to determine whether Planning Permission is required, or whether there is need for an Environmental Impact Assessment if appropriate.

- Prepare application for Outline Planning Permission if appropriate.

- Prepare application for certificates (eg Established Use) if appropriate.

· Submit applications (if instructed by client) with relevant documents, including cheque from client for the appropriate fee.

Inspections/tests

· Make an initial visit to the site and/or existing building. Make photographic record, notes, sketches as appropriate. File information and make an initial appraisal.

· Initiate building or land survey if authorised by client. If independent surveyors are to do this, brief them fully.

· Inspect information provided by client including Health and Safety File if applicable, and check for any reference in previous use or history of site to contamination or presence of hazardous substances, geological problems, underground services etc.

· Advise client, if appropriate, to authorise a special survey to investigate potential health and safety problems.

Contract

· Discuss with the client the procurement methods available and if appropriate explain what the choices would mean.

· Initiate preliminary enquiries about contractors if instructed by client.

Stage input

Information necessary during Stage A–B might include the following as relevant:

- Initial Brief. To include client's requirements, budget, project timetable and timetable for services.

- Information about site and/or existing buildings to be supplied by the client. Legal aspects to be verified by the client's solicitors.

- Further information from client, eg on manufacturing process, equipment, plant layout, accommodation schedule etc.

- Information relating to the user client, eg location, security, particular needs.

- OS maps, site and/or building survey drawings.

- Studies previously undertaken relevant to project, eg social surveys, environmental studies.

- Notes, sketches and photographs made during initial visits.

- Health and Safety File with information on site hazards or references to work carried out previously.

- Contributions, information and recommendations from consultants and specialists if as yet appointed.

- Documents referring to local history of site, political and social context etc (eg as found in library archives or press cuttings).

- Weather records, maps of the area, relevant legal documents etc.

Design and build

- Employer's Requirements as issued to tenderers. *(Contractor Client)*

Stage output

Tangible results/material produced before the conclusion of Stage A–B might include the following as relevant:

- Project Brief developed from the Initial Brief.

- A report to the client on studies to define the feasibility of client's requirements. Analyse and appraise needs, give an environmental assessment and offer possible options, together with recommendations for the way forward. This might include conceptual drawings and diagrams.

- A cost appraisal sufficiently detailed to enable a cost strategy to be devised.

- Where appropriate, a report on the condition of the fabric of an existing (perhaps historic) building, and suggestions for future uses.

- Where appropriate, proposals developed sufficiently to allow an application for Outline Planning Permission.

Design and build

- Initial suggestions for the Employer's Requirements. *(Employer Client)*

- A report to the client on Employer's Requirements as received, and related matters pending preparation of Contractor's Proposals. *(Contractor Client)*

* The initial meetings between client and architect will set the tone for the future working relationship. Clarify your respective roles and responsibilities.

* Establish who exactly the client is. Try to identify a single point of contact as early as possible – preferably named.

* Be properly equipped with information about your practice and its work. Remember that a professional appointment is a process of mutual selection: have ready a practice brochure with details of the practice's track record, personnel and a truthful statement about its expertise, experience and resources.

* Find out whether the client already has some experience of building. Some clients know exactly what is needed and what they can realistically expect from consultants, while some may never have built before – this may be a once in a lifetime experience. Warn the client at once if design requirements, timing and budget seem unrealistic. Explain fully what you advise should be done. Avoid jargon, and take care not to seem patronising or arrogant. Remember that your legal duty of care can relate to the known experience or inexperience of your client.

* Bear in mind that working with a group of people on a community type project, or one which involves a user client, may entail a great deal of extra work, some of it outside normal working hours.

* Consider your reaction to the client and the project. Are you in general sympathy with the client's needs and aspirations – if not, will this have an adverse effect on your work? Are the prospects good for building up a good understanding with the client? A good professional relationship is marked by an atmosphere of trust and a sense of personal service.

* Be clear about the professional services needed. Go carefully and thoroughly through the appointing document. If other consultants and specialists are needed, be prepared to explain their roles and responsibilities. Try to secure that all professional appointments are on mutually interlocking agreements.

* Assess carefully what the project will require in terms of practice resources. Do you have the necessary skills and staff? Can they be made available for the particular programme? If it looks as if you will be overstretched, can you buy in skills or sublet work?

* Get the Agreement down in writing. Maintain the formalities even if the client happens to be an old friend. Use standard forms, preferably without amendments.

* Be strict about keeping to deadlines for reports and other submissions to the client. Set firm dates for approvals, instructions to proceed, and the supply of information. Establish procedures for the client to 'sign off' the brief, design etc at relevant stages.

* Check all information scrupulously; do not make assumptions. Initiate site surveys. Consult the relevant authorities yourself and obtain their advice in writing.

* If you need advice yourself on any matter with which you are unfamiliar or unqualified, consult an appropriate specialist. Never guess or trust to luck.

*   Remember that the law requires a professional to exercise reasonable skill and care. Resist any attempt to get you to guarantee what might not be attainable, eg that a building will be 'fit for the purpose intended'. Do not enter into collateral agreements with third parties or give indemnities which impose greater liabilities than those which arise out of the agreement already entered into with your client.

*   The feasibility report to the client will establish the basis upon which the project should proceed. It may be that the job is not feasible at all, or that the client's requirements, programme and cost limits cannot be reconciled. Make sure your report is comprehensive, soundly researched and positive.

		Tick if relevant	Initial if completed
01	Establish scope, content and context for Stage activities		
02	Check client's written instruction to proceed		
03	Check that previous appointment of architects has been terminated		
04	Check appointing documents wrt services and fees		
05	Open office files and confirm admin procedures		
06	Prepare/adapt project quality plan		
07	Confirm design team and identify leader		
08	Set up in-house project team and identify leader		
09	Check client's project team/personnel/authorised agents		
10	Check office resources wrt services, timetable, fee		
11	Appraise client's requirements, draft Initial Brief		
12	Obtain from client H & S File, other relevant information		
13	Advise client about appointing other consultants, specialists		
14	Agree with other consultants etc methods and procedures		
15	Agree with client consultants' etc services, timetables etc		
16	Advise client on statutory obligations, including H & S		
17	Obtain maps, studies, other contextual material		
18	Discuss with client procurement strategy and options		
19	Make preliminary visit to site/buildings		
20	Advise client about surveys needed and act as authorised		
21	Check relevant legislation and necessary approvals		
22	Check whether other consents might be needed		
23	Consult user clients/third parties as authorised		
24	Monitor office expenditure against fee income		
25	Establish regular report procedures with client		
26	Develop Initial Brief into Project Brief		
27	Collate information from QS, consultants, specialists		
28	Prepare outline planning permission if instructed		
29	Prepare Feasibility Study and Report and submit to client		
30			

Supplement

A-B

A–B/S1   **The briefing process**

A–B/S2   **Project brief checklist**

A–B/S3   **Design team appointments and working**

A–B/S4   **Planning permission, other consents and approvals**

A–B/S5   **Health and safety checklists**

A–B/S6   **A project quality plan**

A–B/S7   **Inspecting the site**

A–B/S8   **Financial appraisal**

The briefing process

Compiling the brief and developing the design are activities which interact as shown in Fig D.01. Briefing is really a continuous process through to Detail Design, but for convenience it can be regarded as evolving through four distinct phases. The Client's Requirements are the starting point, and it should never be forgotten that the client is at the core of the process. An inexperienced client, perhaps on a smaller size project, might welcome the assistance of the architect in preparing Client's Requirements.

The briefing process must be appropriate to the nature of the project. Some projects might depend upon planning and space standards which have already been widely researched and are generally available. Other projects might require considerable original investigation and extensive design studies. Such factors are likely to influence both the cost and duration of the design process and the development of the brief.

The Client's Requirements

The Client's Requirements will first need to be evaluated to determine whether they provide an adequate statement. They should set out the objectives which the client wishes to achieve in the project, and will probably refer to functional requirements, environmental standards, levels of quality, life span and maintenance. After evaluation and discussion these Requirements may need to be adapted or modified to form the Initial Brief.

The Initial Brief

The Initial Brief may be anything from a broad preliminary statement of interest to a comprehensive set of technical requirements. It will rarely be sufficiently clear or detailed for design work, but it should be seen as the basis for feasibility studies. Considerable further investigation and development work may be necessary to bring it to the level of a Project Brief by the end of Stage A–B. However, it should be seen as an important part of developing the brief, and as such should be a formalised document to be agreed with the client.

The Project Brief

The Project Brief should be a document which covers the technical, managerial and design intentions as set out in the Initial Brief, and shows how these requirements are to be met. It is likely to be the result of research and development involving all the design team, with additional expertise and advice from commissioned specialists. It will be the outcome of activities such as:
· feasibility studies;
· site or building survey and studies;
· research into functional needs;
· environmental impact considerations;
· statutory constraints;
· cost appraisal studies.

The Project Brief should be seen as a starting point for the development of the Design Brief and should be formalised by the end of Stage A–B.

The Design Brief

The Design Brief, developed from the Project Brief, should define all design requirements. It should be prepared by the architect in collaboration with the client, and with coordinated contributions from all consultants and specialists, and the health and safety Planning Supervisor. Development of this Design Brief will probably require:

- assembly of all relevant information;
- design studies and investigations;
- preparation of an outline design proposal;
- preparation of a cost plan.

The Design Brief is the foundation on which the design will develop, and serves as a yardstick against which further design development can be measured. As such it is a factual record, and a document of importance.

The Consolidated Brief

The Consolidated Brief is the last stage in the briefing process and may be equated with the end of Plan of Work Stage D. It will be the basis for further detailed design work, and should take the form of a report to client containing the following:

- introduction, purpose, résumé of brief development;
- summary of research undertaken;
- discussion of design options and conclusions;
- description of proposed scheme design;
- cost plan and programme.

The Consolidated Brief should be 'signed off' by the client after approval.

The four steps outlined above are likely to be found in most projects of reasonable substance or complexity.

The briefing process is something that should always be developed systematically. It provides the framework within which the design can be developed, and it is an indispensable part of quality management. However, on projects of a more domestic scale the design and briefing processes might be compressed. Nevertheless, sufficient time should be allowed for this work to be done thoroughly, and architects should resist jumping to quick design solutions which might not meet the client's requirements.

The process of brief development is cyclical, and it should be accepted that clients sometimes wish to modify their requirements even after approval of the Consolidated Brief. Major changes could lead to the abandoning of design work already completed, or at least have a significant effect upon cost, time and statutory consents. It is therefore essential to have an identifiable approved Consolidated Brief to start with, and to have a procedure for Brief Change Control as part of the quality management plan. This will enable the client to be aware of the implications of changes to the Consolidated Brief before final instructions are given.

Project brief checklist

A Project Brief checklist relevant at the end of Stage A–B might include the following:

General

- Client's objectives, Requirements and established priorities and criteria;
- quality standards;
- life expectancy of building and components;
- user client considerations;
- security requirements;
- budgets for security, energy, maintenance including cleaning (ie costs in use);
- detailed functional requirements of direct client/user client;
- site history and topography;
- preferred spatial relationships and orientation;
- studies previously commissioned;
- plans for future expansion;
- exact location of boundaries;
- other parties known to have expressed an interest, eg English Heritage, Royal Fine Arts Commission etc.

Planning and building considerations

- Known constraints arising from previous consents or conditions;
- likelihood of planning gain or Section 106 Agreement;
- impact of Local Development Plan;
- leasehold/freehold interests and party walls, rights of light, access or other known easements.

Environmental

- Services below ground and known restrictions on development;
- likely parking requirements;
- likelihood of archaeological or antiquarian discoveries;
- known road widening or development plans;
- known problems with the site, eg geological conditions, hazardous substances.

Financial

- Funding or institutional requirements or restrictions;
- approximate cost per sq ft if speculative development;
- grants, subsidies, or information relating to tax advantages (eg VAT).

Appointments

When acting as lead consultant, the architect should advise the client on the appointment of other consultants and specialists as necessary. The appointment and payment of consultants and specialists are matters best dealt with directly by the client; the services required should be identified in detail and recorded. The conditions of appointment for all consultants should be compatible and preferably to a common basis.

It is very important for the architect to know precisely what is included in the appointment terms of all consultants, so as to be able to minimise any overlap or duplication and to coordinate effectively the work of all the members of the design team. It is also desirable to ensure that all members are appointed under compatible conditions with a common policy concerning responsibilities, insurance, collateral agreements etc.

The Latham Report, *Constructing the Team*, published in 1994, contained significant recommendations for a family of compatible documents to include the appointment of consultants, contractors and subcontractors. At the time of writing (1995), these are under discussion by the various bodies who at present publish documents related to their own immediate interests. References in this edition of the *Architect's Job Book* are to appointing documents currently in use.

Depending on the nature and size of the project, a wide range of specialists and/or consultants may be needed at some stage. For example:

Surveyors
- Quantity surveyor
- Land surveyor
- Building surveyor
- Party wall surveyor.

Engineering consultants
- Civil engineer (including geotechnics)
- Structural engineer.

Building services consultants
- Heating and ventilating engineer
- Electrical engineer
- Lighting consultant.

Other consultants and specialists
- Planning Supervisor
- Landscape consultant
- Acoustic consultant
- Conservator
- Health and safety consultant
- Fire engineering consultant
- Public health consultant
- Drainage consultant
- Interior design consultant
- Facilities management consultant
- Security adviser.

Of these, the appointments most likely to be relevant at Stage A–B are:

Quantity surveyors
Standard conditions of engagement are published by the Royal Institution of Chartered Surveyors (RICS) relating to a wide range of services. These need to be examined carefully to establish which services are to be provided for the particular appointment.

Structural engineers
Standard conditions of engagement and a number of different forms of agreement are published by the Association of Consulting Engineers (ACE). Normal services for structural work are arranged broadly in accordance with the Plan of Work stages. These need to be examined carefully to establish which services are to be provided for the particular appointment.

Building services engineers

Standard conditions of engagement are published by the Association of Consulting Engineers. The basic range of services can include for Full Duties, Abridged Duties, or Performance Duties. The conditions need to be examined carefully to establish which services are to be provided for the particular appointment.

With engineering services, architects are reminded that:

(a) 'working drawings' as understood in architectural terminology are not produced by M & E consultants;

(b) 'builders work' drawings are for the architect to arrange, making sure that requirements for holes, shafts, access, insulation etc are properly coordinated and integrated into the design;

(c) 'coordination drawings', where commissioned, should show detailed layouts and their relationship to plant rooms, spaces, structure etc;

(d) 'installation drawings' (or 'shop drawings') are produced by the subcontractors or suppliers, and may be expected to show only general lines of pipework, fabrication, and equipment installation details for comment by the engineering services consultant prior to fabrication or installation.

It is normally the architect's responsibility to coordinate and integrate the work of consultants and specialists into the overall design. To this end, architects will need to inspect drawings submitted by specialists. However, contract documents should clearly place the responsibility for coordination of work being carried out on site with the main contractor.

Design team roles and responsibilities

Quantity surveyor

The QS can assist the architect in assessing special site and other problems such as access, topography, economic site use and working. He can analyse cost information on other similar projects, local levels of building costs and cost trends etc, and can judge whether the client's budget is realistic and compatible with other stated requirements.

The QS should cooperate with the Planning Supervisor, liaise with other consultants and specialists, attend design team meetings, and prepare the financial appraisal for the feasibility report.

Structural engineer

The structural engineer can advise the architect about local conditions relevant to the site, such as soil and geotechnical factors, roads, sewers, water supply etc. He can:

· obtain existing information and interpret it;

· identify hazards and hazardous substances;

· arrange for site, structural and drainage surveys;

· advise on alternative structural solutions;

· prepare cost planning information for the QS;

· prepare design criteria and calculations;

· advise on structural aspects of party walls, temporary structures and demolition work.

He should cooperate with the Planning Supervisor, liaise with other consultants and specialists, attend design team meetings, and contribute to the feasibility report.

Building services engineers

The mechanical and electrical engineers should cooperate with the Planning Supervisor, and liaise with the architect and structural engineer to study climatic conditions, energy use and conservation, emission problems etc, and should consult relevant authorities as necessary.

The M & E engineers can:
- provide details of load and space requirements for services;
- prepare feasibility studies, estimates, forecasts and maintenance cost options;
- assist in dealings with statutory bodies;
- prepare outline schemes;
- prepare energy management studies and report;
- prepare design criteria, and calculations;
- advise on installation options and cost implications;
- advise on energy, cost/benefit, and running costs.

They should attend design team meetings, and contribute to the feasibility report.

Design team meetings

The design team will probably need to be enlarged during the development of the project. However, it is essential that it is formally constituted with proper definition of responsibility and clearly accepted roles. Regular design team meetings are important to review progress and to record decisions. A specimen agenda for the initial design team meeting is shown as Fig AB.04, and although the list of items will need modifying as the project progresses, the main headings should remain consistent throughout. In this way the history of each aspect of job administration will be automatically recorded and can be easily traced.

A system of regular reporting can be established. For example, the client's representative will report under the heading 'Brief', the architect under 'Site' and 'Approvals', the quantity surveyor under 'Cost control', and so on. It is assumed that an architect acting as lead consultant or design team leader will chair such meetings.

Fig AB.04   **Specimen agenda for initial design team meeting**

1 **Design team and reports**
   Appointments, personnel
   Roles and responsibilities
   Lines of communication for policy/day to day matters
   Pattern and reporting procedures for future meetings
   Project programme
   Team members' programmes and progress

2 **Brief**
   Client's requirements
   Development of brief
   Changes to brief, implications and control procedures
   Pattern and procedures for reporting to client
   Preparation of Stage reports to client

3 **Site**
   Information from client about site, foreseeable hazards
   Assessment of risks
   Development constraints, physical and statutory
   Surveys and consents

4 **Approvals**
   Private individuals/bodies
   Town and country planning
   Building Regulations
   Fire officer
   Legal (eg adjoining owners)

5 **Design and cost control**
   Concepts
   - feasibility assessment
   - development of the brief
   Coordination of design team effort
   - general design
   - structures
   - services
   Drawings
   - agreed methods, scales, software, referencing
   - distribution procedures
   Budget
   - development of cost plan
   - variations

6 **Contract**
   Priorities and phasing
   Programming
   Procurement
   Tendering procedures and documents, health and safety plan:
   - main contract
   - subcontracts

7 **Any other business**

8 **Date of next meeting**

Planning permission, other consents and approvals   A–B/S4

Consents may have to be obtained during Stages A–B, C, D and F from authorities, organisations or persons having jurisdiction over or rights affecting the project, or who are affected by the project. Consents which could affect feasibility should be applied for during Stage A–B.

Depending on the nature of the project, the site, and the amount of information available, each application for consent should be made at the earliest possible time in order to avoid abortive work.

Before initiating applications for consents:
· explain fully to the client what consents are necessary and what is likely to be involved;
· discover whether the client has contacts or lines of communication with authorities or individuals concerned;
· inform the client about fees payable direct by him;
· inform the client about the likely timescale for processing applications and the degree of consultation;
· make it clear to the client that architects do not *obtain* consents, this being beyond their power, but that they prepare submissions or make application on behalf of their clients in accordance with the agreement for professional services.

Check planning situation

Discover or confirm:
· whether there is an earlier planning permission for the site;
· whether planning permission is required;
· whether any statutory Development Plan is applicable to the area, eg Structure Plan, Local Plan, or Unitary Development Plan;
· whether the proposals constitute 'Change of Use' under the Use Classes Order;
· whether the proposals are within a Designated Urban Development Corporation, Enterprise or Simplified Planning Zone;
· whether the proposals are likely to be the subject of planning gain or other matters under a Section 106 agreement.

Check relevant procedures

Check which of the following procedures are relevant:
· Application to determine whether planning application is necessary
· Application for certificate of established use
· Application for mining or working of minerals
· Application for hazardous substances consent
· Application for outline planning permission
· Application for full planning permission to develop land
· Application for listed building consent
· Application for conservation area consent
· Application for approval of 'conditions' on a planning permission
· Application for varying or discharging conditions attached to listed building consent or conservation area consent
· Application for varying or revoking conditions attached to a planning permission
· Application for approval of reserved matters following an outline planning permission
· Application for a scheduled monument consent
· Application for a certificate of immunity from listing
· Application to fell or lop a tree
· Notification under Circular 18/84 for Crown or local authority development
· Application to establish the need for an Environmental Assessment.

It should be noted that signs and advertisements may be subject to the Control of Advertisement Regulations. Some advertisements may be exempt from control, some may be displayed with deemed consent, while others will require the express consent of the local planning authority.

The planning application

Make preparations
· Prepare all documentation on the assumption that it might serve as supporting evidence in an Appeal.
· Confirm by letter all meetings, phone calls etc with the planning authority.
· Make sure that the client's representative also attends all critical meetings with the planning authority.
· At an early stage consider project presentations to attract the interest and support of neighbourhood and parish groups, appropriate lobbies and news media.

Check the following:
· dates of planning meetings;
· probable date by which decision is to be given;
· number and types of drawings required;
· procedures, eg notices in the press, site notices etc.

When making a planning application, check that:
· forms are carefully completed. Identify or list submitted drawings on forms or in covering letter;
· an accurate site plan identifies the land concerned, clearly defined in red;
· a covering letter accompanies the application, explaining features of the scheme;
· an Ownership Certificate A (or B, C, D as appropriate) is served;
· a cheque from the client for the appropriate sum is submitted at the same time (having checked the correct amount with the planning authority, as it usually increases year on year);
· the application is date-stamped by the planning authority (this defines the start of the period for determination);
· a copy of the written report by the Planning Officer to the Planning Committee is obtained;
· if permitted and appropriate, oral representation is made to the Planning Committee.

The planning meeting
If appropriate, attend critical meetings with the client's representative. Arrange for a shorthand note to be taken by another person. If planning permission is refused and an Appeal is contemplated, send your account of proceedings to the Chief Executive of the authority. If not dissented from, it may have the status of 'agreed notes'. Examine the agenda and record of the meeting; these may constitute the basis for an Appeal.

Checklists

ROADS AND HIGHWAYS

Discover or confirm:
- whether there are relevant construction or improvement schemes;
- building lines and improvement lines;
- loading restrictions, special access requirements for exceptional loads;
- street lighting requirements;
- requirements for road and pavement widths, access cross-overs, turning circles, sight lines etc;
- requirements for stopping up or diverting highway;
- requirements for bridging over highways;
- restrictions on hoardings, site working.

DRAINAGE AND MAINS SUPPLY SERVICES

1 Discover or confirm the following drainage systems affecting the project.

Public drainage –
to sewer combined with surface water
to separate soil and surface water sewers
to soil sewers and soakaways for surface water
to watercourse for surface water etc.

Private drainage –
to cesspool, septic tank, treatment plant

2 Check the following drainage details:
- positions, sizes, invert levels and direction of flow for all sewers on or immediately adjacent to the site;
- lowest levels at which connections may be made;
- methods of connection possible and whether local authority or contractor is to make connections;
- whether interceptor traps are required;
- particular requirements concerning internal drainage.

3 Check with water supply company or authority:
- particular regulations and requirements;
- location, depth, size and pressure of mains on or near site;
- requirements for intake, stopcocks, metering etc.

4 Check with gas supply company or authority:
- permanent and temporary supplies;
- location, depth and size of mains on or near site;
- requirements for intake, stopcocks, metering etc.

5 Check with electricity supply company or authority:
- permanent and temporary supplies (give estimate of loads required);
- voltage and capacity of existing cables;
- whether a substation will be required;
- location and clearance of cables, towers and overhead lines on or near site;
- position of intake ducts.

6 Check with telecommunications/cable company or authority:
- permanent and temporary services;
- location and clearance of underground cables and pole lines on or near site;
- position of intake ducts.

7 Procedures to follow where relevant:
- Check dates by which applications for supply services have to be made to fit project programme.
- Confirm what information is required by and from the supply company or authority concerned.
- Obtain necessary forms for client to approve and sign as supply consumer.

OTHER CONSENTS

1 Check what other consents are required from national bodies. These may arise from central or regional policies and be connected with:
- Royal Fine Arts Commission
- Housing Corporation
- English Heritage (and comparable organisations for Wales and Scotland)
- National Rivers Authority/British Waterways Board
- National Trust
- National Parks Authority.

2 Check what enquiries are advisable from agents acting for estate offices, landlords, lessees, tenants or adjoining owners and whether consents are required in connection with:
- boundaries
- party walls
- easements (eg air, light, way)
- covenants (restrictive or otherwise).

3 Check what statutory consents might be relevant to particular types of projects, such as:
- licensed premises and restaurants
- cinemas and theatres
- sports stadia
- petrol stations
- abbattoirs
- music and dance halls
- residential nursing homes
- health buildings and clinics.

Health and safety checklists

Legislation

The principal legislation is the Health and Safety at Work etc Act 1974, which sets out general duties on the part of both employers and employees. These were reinforced with the introduction of the Management of Health and Safety at Work Regulations 1992.

The Workplace (Health, Safety and Welfare) Regulations 1992 are relevant at Stage A–B. Although they place a duty on employers in respect of workplaces under their control, there are implications for the way in which new workplaces are designed and fitted out. This can be in respect of planning (eg traffic routes, escalators, room dimensions, sanitary provisions etc); finishes (eg floors, wall surfaces); and installations (eg lighting, heating, ventilation). The Regulations are concerned not only with the initial provision of safe conditions for staff but also with safety for cleaning and maintenance.

The RIBA has published a safety code for personnel visiting building sites (see Fig AB.05) and this should be issued to staff and strictly observed.

The Construction (Design and Management) Regulations 1994 ('the CDM Regulations') implement an EC Directive which requires that account be taken of the general principles of prevention concerning safety and health during the stages of project design organisation, construction and future maintenance. The Regulations impose duties on the Client, Designer, Planning Supervisor and Principal Contractor. They apply to nearly all projects where construction work will be of more than 30 days duration or where more than 500 person days of construction work are involved, except in the case of domestic clients undertaking work on their own residences solely for their own occupation.

The architect's role

The architect, when acting as lead consultant or 'Designer' (as referred to in the CDM Regulations) should carefully study the text of the Regulations and the Approved Code of Practice. It would also be wise to check the following.

· Check that the client is aware of his legal duty to appoint a Planning Supervisor 'as soon as practicable', and a principal contractor. He must be satisfied as to the competence and resources of both concerning health and safety matters.
· Check that the client is aware of his legal duty to make available a Health and Safety File in respect of work previously carried out, and other relevant information concerning the site or premises.
· Check that inspections and surveys of site or buildings cover all matters which might indicate potential health and safety hazards. This is a 'Designer's' duty, and if a detailed survey is thought necessary, the client must be prepared to pay for it.
· Check that when undertaking risk assessments, proper consideration is given to eliminating or reducing potential health and safety hazards when planning site layouts or development. This will include the way that the contractor's operations on site are to be planned.
· Check that there is full cooperation between the lead consultant and all others having a design input (including consultants and specialist subcontractors) with regard to health and safety matters.
· Check that there is full cooperation with the Planning Supervisor over the production of information which may be relevant for the pre-tender Health and Safety Plan.
· Check that the Planning Supervisor is invited to attend design team meetings, and to comment as appropriate.
· Check that in all design development the issues of safe specification, safe buildability, and maintenance are kept fully in mind.

Fig AB.05   **Visits to sites and unoccupied buildings: RIBA safety code**

Health and Safety legislation lays clear obligations on clients, designers, and principal contractors. The following code is complementary advice to all architects engaged in visits to buildings and sites.
Visits to building sites, unoccupied buildings and construction operations can be potentially dangerous. Consider the likely hazards. Follow the safety code.

1   Occupied building sites

● The Contractor or occupier has a responsibility for the safety of persons lawfully on site. Do not enter sites or buildings without permission, and immediately report to the person in charge. Comply with all requests from the contractor, his representative or other supervisory staff. See the contractor when you arrive, and when you leave the site.

● Wear suitable clothing, in particular protective headgear (a hard hat) and stout shoes or boots. Do not wear thin-soled or slippery shoes. Avoid loose clothes which might catch on an obstruction.

● Check that ladders are securely fixed and that planks are secure. Beware of overhead projections, scaffolding and plant, and proceed with caution. Particular care is necessary in windy, cold, wet or muddy conditions. Keep clear of excavations and beware of openings in floors etc. Do not lean on guard rails, scaffoldings etc. Do not interfere with any temporary barriers, guard rails or lights. Beware of ladders on which the rungs may have rusted or rotted, and never climb a ladder which is not securely fixed at the top.

● Do not touch any plant or equipment. Keep clear of machinery and stacked materials. Watch out for temporary cables, pumps, hoses and electric fittings.

● Do not walk and look around at the same time. Keep one hand free at all times when moving. Make sure that you are in a safe and balanced position whenever making notes or taking photographs.

● Report to the contractor anything that comes to your notice on the site as being unsafe.

2   Unoccupied buildings and sites

● As a general rule do not visit an empty building or unoccupied site on your own. Make sure that someone knows where you are, and at what time you expect to return.

● Do not take chances. Do not visit an empty building if you think it unsafe. Do not visit an unoccupied site if you think it dangerous. Anticipate hazards. Common dangers include:
– the possibility of partial or total structural collapse
– rotten or insecure floors and stairs
– hidden pits, ducts, openings etc, fragile construction, eg asbestos or plastic sheets on roofs
– space which has not been used or ventilated for some time
– live services
– contamination by chemicals or asbestos
– Intruders who may still be around
– contamination by vermin or birds, or poisonous substances put down to control them.

● Plan the visit and make sure that you take with you appropriate equipment and protective clothing. Apart from stout shoes and a hard hat, remember that unoccupied buildings can be dirty, damp, cold and dark; so go prepared.

● Familiarise yourself beforehand with the plan of the building, particularly the exit routes. Make sure that security devices on exits will allow you to reach safety quickly.

● Look for defects in the floors ahead, eg wet areas, holes, materials that might be covering up holes.

● Walk over the structural members (eg joists, beams, etc) whenever possible – do not rely on floorboards alone.

● Do not walk and look around at the same time. Keep one hand free at all times when moving. Do not walk and try to take notes at the same time. Make sure that you are in a safe and balanced position when taking photographs or stretching out to take measurements.

● Check on protection when approaching stairwells, lift shafts, roof perimeters, etc.

● Do not assume that services (eg cables, sockets, pipes, etc) are safe or have been isolated.

● If you suspect the presence of gas, inflammable liquids, dangerous chemicals or free asbestos fibre leave the building immediately.

● If you sustain cuts, penetration by nails or other serious injury, seek immediate medical advice.

● Always heed these three golden rules:
– do not rush
– if uncertain do not proceed – seek advice or assistance
– do not smoke or use naked flame.

· Check that the pre-tender Health and Safety Plan is part of the tender documentation supplied to the principal contractor and subcontractors.
· Check that tenders are carefully examined to make sure that the selected Principal Contractor has the necessary competence and resources available to deal with health and safety matters, and that price and programme reflect this.
· Check that the building contract has provisions for compliance with Health and Safety Regulations, and for the contractor to cooperate with the Planning Supervisor and provide 'as built' information etc.
· Check that the client is aware that no work must start on site before a construction phase Health and Safety Plan has been produced by the Principal Contractor as a management document for the works.
· Check that a copy of any architect's instruction or variation with health and safety implications is passed to the Planning Supervisor, so that the Health and Safety Plan can be updated accordingly.
· Check that relevant information is passed to the Planning Supervisor from time to time for possible inclusion in the Health and Safety File.

The Planning Supervisor

Where this function is discharged by the architect on smaller contracts, it should be seen as a separate appointment, made via a separate appointing document and with an identifiable separate fee.

Where an independent Planning Supervisor is to be appointed, an architect not otherwise involved in the job might be a suitable person. In all cases such appointments should only be considered by architects who have undergone proper training, fully understand the risks, and have appropriate insurance cover.

Lead consultants or design team leaders working on a project where an independent Planning Supervisor has been appointed would do well to check that this appointee:
· gives proper notice to the Health and Safety Executive initially;
· cooperates effectively in structuring information for a pre-tender Health and Safety Plan;
· is thorough over the evaluation of health and safety aspects of the Principal Contractors' tenders, and is prepared to advise the client impartially;
· is thorough but reasonable in evaluating the acceptability of the construction phase Health and Safety Plan from the Principal Contractor and as updated from time to time;
· will prepare the statutory Health and Safety File for deposit with the client at the conclusion of construction, and will explain to the client his obligations concerning its safekeeping and future use.

These may not be statutory duties, but such checks are very much in the spirit of the legislation and certainly demonstrate the use of reasonable skill and care.

The Health and Safety Notice

This notice, which is a statutory requirement, is normally submitted by the Planning Supervisor to the Health and Safety Executive. It should include the particulars listed below, as they become known.
· Date of forwarding.
· Address of construction site.
· Name and address of client.
· Type of project.
· Name and address of Planning Supervisor.

- Declaration confirming appointment of Planning Supervisor.
- Name and address of Principal Contractor (when appointed).
- Declaration confirming appointment of Principal Contractor.
- Date for commencement of construction (when known).
- Contract period for construction (when known).
- Estimated maximum number of workforce.
- Total number of contractors (ie Principal Contractor and nominated/approved subcontractors) expected on site.
- Names and addresses of nominated/approved subcontractors already selected.

The Health and Safety Plan

The Health and Safety Plan, a document for which the Planning Supervisor should assume responsibility pre-tender, and for which the Principal Contractor is responsible, at construction phase might include the information listed below.
- Name of client.
- Nature of construction work and expected timetable.
- Existing environment (eg land uses, planning restrictions, services which might have health and safety implications, traffic systems and restrictions which might affect site working).
- Ground conditions and possible hazards.
- Existing buildings: possible hazards, instability problems, special health problems associated with materials etc.
- Health and Safety File particulars from previous works, supplied by client/owner.
- Design principles (eg structural design precautions), risk hazards which are unavoidable etc.
- Construction information and choice of materials likely to cause health hazards and which cannot be avoided.
- Site access, egress, organisation of working.
- Particular precautions where exclusive possession is not available.
- Procedures for dealing with unforeseeable circumstances, and updates to Health and Safety Plan.

The Health and Safety File

The Health and Safety File, a document for which the Planning Supervisor should assume responsibility, is to be deposited with the client at the completion of the contract. It will probably be assembled from information acquired gradually and steadily as the works progress. The client might need briefing as to its purpose, safekeeping, and future use.

The File will be part record and part maintenance manual. It should include the following.
- Design criteria.
- General details of constructional systems and methods, materials used, and any potentially hazardous aspects.
- Record drawings (as built).
- Details of equipment, finishes, and maintenance facilities (eg window cleaning).
- Maintenance procedures for the structure and finishes, including details and schedules by manufacturers and installers.
- Operating instructions and maintenance manuals produced by consultants, subcontractors and suppliers for services installations, with recommendations for renewal and replacement cycle of plant and equipment.
- Information on location, setting and servicing of all services installations including alarms.

References in this *Architect's Job Book* to setting up and developing a project quality plan are made with the BS 5750 definition of Quality Management and Quality Systems in mind.

At the time of writing, a number of architects' practices have certified 'Quality Assured' status, and these will already be operating a system which includes for project quality plans.

Many practices have systematic procedures, whether or not they describe these as 'quality management', which constitute an effective framework for running the office and the individual jobs. There will probably be an office handbook or manual where the procedural framework is clearly set out. In addition to the office organisation, policy and review mechanism, the manual will probably describe general administrative procedures, the way appointments are to be formalised, job costing and fees, employing consultants, dealing with correspondence, management of design, producing and issuing drawings, administering contracts and keeping records. These and other matters are all part of the way a methodical practice carries on its business.

The system as described in the manual should be available to all staff, and parts could be made available to a client. A quality system will describe:
- what the practice aims to offer in respect of services;
- how the practice is organised and managed so as to meet those aims;
- what measures the practice adopts to inspect, test, and keep its activities under review;
- what steps the practice takes if corrective action is required in the event of non-conforming activities.

Quality management is concerned with consistent performance to stated requirements, and the system is essentially one of control.

Although a practice's quality manual will cover most aspects of its quality system, there will also be project quality plans setting out the way the system is applied to the particular project. A project quality plan will probably, although not necessarily, be a stand-alone document in hard copy as well as software, written or diagrammatic. Many of the procedures might be described in detail elsewhere (eg in the manual or other documents, such as this *Architect's Job Book*) and could be included by reference.

A typical project quality plan might include:

Project description
- Client's design requirements;
- synopsis of brief and priorities;
- intended life span of building overall and of components;
- constraints which arise from legislation or other sources.

Project organisation
- Identity of client and representatives;
- identified practice/project quality manager;
- agreed procedures for consultations/approvals;
- principal practice staff assigned to the project and their defined responsibilities;
- project timetable/programmes.

Project team
- Consultants/specialists with design input;
- defined responsibilities, including review procedures;
- management, procedures for administration, including coordination.

Control procedures
- Brief development control, and reviews;
- design input control, design management and development, and patterns of design review;
- design and information output control;
- project specification basis and development;
- project administration and document control procedures;
- procurement, and procedures for appointment of the project construction team;
- contract administration procedures;
- monitoring of contractors' quality management.

Change control
- Agreed procedures for modifications or changes to approved brief;
- agreed procedures for modifications or changes to approved designs;
- records of modifications or changes;
- identification of documents subjected to revision and withdrawal to prevent unintended use.

Tests
- Programme for inspections and tests, and personnel involved;
- procedures and check sheets or reports to be used;
- corrective action in the event of non-conforming work;
- programme for audits, personnel involved, and audit reports.

Particular instructions
- Those items in practice's general quality plan to be expressly excluded in the case of this particular project;
- items not covered by general quality plan to be specifically included in the case of this particular project.

Records
- End of project reviews;
- experience feedback studies and reports;
- maintenance manuals and operating instructions;
- as built information;
- job records and files.

To summarise, a project quality plan will be in the form most appropriate for the particular project. It should be a document which:
- defines activities and how they are to be carried out;
- should be adequate for submission to a client at fee bidding stage if required, or sufficient to offer to a client later for acceptance and review;
- is reviewed regularly through the progress of the project, with amendments and revisions as necessary submitted for acceptance before implementation.

The amount of detail included will vary, depending on how much has already been set out in the practice's quality plan.

Proper inspections and surveys of sites and existing buildings are essential at Stage A–B and are best done by architects themselves. Rough preliminary surveys are not good enough and are an inadequate basis on which to judge feasibility. Ill-founded recommendations at this stage can lead to serious problems later.

When considering survey action, try to establish:
· the kind of survey needed and precisely what is to be surveyed;
· who will carry out the survey – the practice's own staff, external land or building surveyors, other specialists;
· who will pay for the survey and where liability will rest in the event of errors.

Identify the boundaries of the site to be surveyed or the limits of the building. Confirm with the client that access will be available and obtain keys if necessary. Notify persons on site as appropriate.

Do not overlook statutory obligations arising, particularly those concerning Occupiers Liability, and Health and Safety. Always heed the RIBA Safety Code for occupied building sites and unoccupied buildings and sites (see Fig AB.05).

Information about immediate area

Check:
· general context and character, outstanding visual features;
· local development plan, action area plans, construction work currently under way;
· evidence of social and economic patterns;
· traffic movement patterns, noise, pollution;
· derelict areas, nearby black spots, visually detracting features.

Visual inspection of site

Check:
· aspect, orientation, shelter, overshadowing from adjacent buildings or trees;
· hedges, ditches, ponds, wet/soft patches, underground streams;
· benchmarks, contours, and slope of site;
· paths, gates, stiles which might indicate rights of way;
· overhead cables, pylons and poles;
· possible health and safety hazards, eg flooding, exposure, unsafe trees etc;
· properties adjoining the site, their condition, usage, evidence of subsidence, fire risks, party walls etc;
· possible health and safety hazards such as radon or other gases, pollutants and contamination from previous use, filled basements etc;
· adjacent waterways, railways, busy roads;
· possible restrictions on site access, delivery or site working;
· possible restrictions due to sensitive building uses adjacent, eg hospital, nursery school, law court.

Site survey information

If the site survey is to be undertaken by a surveying firm, make sure that this is agreed with the client as not part of the architect's services, and is to be paid for direct. Confirm:
· by whom the surveyors are to be engaged;
· how the surveying fees are to be paid;
· who is doing which part of the work;
· how the results are to be presented;
· arrangements for access, security, protection and insurance.

If appropriate arrange for a survey of tree species and condition and an analysis of top soil.

The information presented in the survey plans and reports might be expected to include the following.

Plans, showing:
· existing and proposed boundaries;
· outline of existing buildings and roads;
· boundary fences, access ways, garden and adjacent walls, their height, profile, material, ownership and condition;
· ditches, ponds, waterways above or below ground;
· wet or bad patches (discover seasonal variations from local sources);
· rock outcrops and other geological features, their type and size;
· position of trial holes;
· rights of way/access (check with client's solicitors, local authority).

Sections, drawn on separate sheets taken along the full length of section lines on the key drawings, to the same scale as the plan.

Levels, showing:
· position and level of benchmarks or basis of datum;
· calculated levels in true relationship to an ordnance datum level;
· spot levels on a 10m grid related to ordnance survey grid, or closer where local variations occur, eg at changes of level, hillocks etc.

Spot levels, indicating:
· the base of all trees;
· all services covers etc;
· pavement kerbs and road crowns where they enter site.

Indicate contours, intervals (in metres) and position of section lines (on grid lines where possible).

Indicate all services above and below ground adjacent to, connecting into or crossing the site with relevant levels, falls, heights, access points, manholes (show cover levels and inverts). Also:
· pylons, posts (show headroom);
· soil and surface water drains;
· water mains;
· electricity cables;
· telecommunication cables;
· gas mains;
· any other services.

Indicate trees, hedges and large shrubs, their height and position, spread of branches and diameter of trunk 1m above ground level.

Soil investigations

On a domestic project or one which involves a relatively small and light structure, it might well be sufficient for the architect to instruct the digging of trial pits. These should be set out with regard to the siting of the proposed building. On anything larger, investigation by boreholes may be necessary to obtain information and data for the design and construction of foundations, underground structures, road works, earthworks etc.

The structural consultant may be able to give preliminary advice by examining available information about the geology and history of the site, eg maps and memos produced by the Institute of Geological Sciences, Ordnance Survey maps, engineering data from earlier works in the area, aerial photographs.

The consultant should recommend the type and extent of investigation and the number of trial holes necessary to obtain an accurate assessment of the subsoil and water table conditions.

The investigating firm must allow for carrying out the work in accordance with any special requirements of the existing owners or occupiers of the site. They and/or their subcontractor specialists should be made responsible for all security, protection and related insurance during execution of the work.

The field work should be supervised by the engineer, and daily liaison should be maintained so that any variations indicated by the borehole findings can be made. Daily site records should be sent to the engineer stating:
· borehole numbers and location;
· date and times of boring;
· type of plant and method of boring;
· diameter of boring casing and core;
· description of strata and depth of base of each stratum;
· level at bottom of casing when sample taken, or in situ test carried out on each core drilled;
· depths at which each sample was taken and in situ tests made;
· water levels.

On completing the site work, the contractor should submit to the engineer preliminary borehole logs together with a list of samples so that instructions can be given for laboratory testing.

The final site investigation should be submitted as a draft (for approval of its form, not content). Unless otherwise specified it should contain:
· description of work carried out (ie site and laboratory work);
· borehole logs;
· laboratory test results, including geological classification, index properties, acidity, sulphate content etc;
· records of water levels in standpipes and/or piezometers installed in boreholes, with notes of any variations;
· results of strength tests;
· diagrammatic cross-section through site showing trial holes related to a datum and assumed connecting geological structure, water table etc;
· plan showing position of trial holes, incorporated with main survey plan if appropriate.

Surveys of existing buildings

It is essential that the architect personally walks through every room in the building to be surveyed, regardless of whether the survey is being done by in-house personnel or by a surveying firm. It is important to perceive the architectural character of a building and the way it has been constructed.

The measured survey drawings might show:
· plans, sections, elevations;
· elevational features, eg plinths, string courses, openings;
· precise levels at floors, datum, thickness and construction;
· levels of external ground;
· details of decoration, profiles, false columns etc;
· finishes and colours;
· loose equipment, landlord's fittings etc.

A written report might include information that cannot be shown graphically, such as:
· structural and other defects and their causes;
· dry rot, damp penetration, condensation;
· infestation by rodents, beetles and other insects;
· recent repairs and decoration;
· settlement cracks, mis-shapen openings, gaps at skirtings and windows;
· walls that are misaligned or have bulges;
· sagging roofs, defective roof coverings;
· deflection of beams or lintels, cracks at beam bearings.

The architects/surveyors should state whether or not they were able to see inside the structure of the building and how much they were able to see. It is important not to infer the state of the whole building from sight of one part of it. A statement on the following lines should appear at the end of the relevant part of the report (as stipulated in most professional indemnity insurance policies):

'It has not been possible to make a detailed examination of the floor or roof construction except at the positions described because material damage would have been caused in gaining access. It is therefore impossible to make any statement about the condition of the unexamined structure.'

Where appropriate, the client should be advised to call in specialists, eg mechanical, electrical, timber treatment, and should be asked for instructions regarding any fees, expenses and inconvenience arising from their investigations.

A–B/S8　Financial appraisal

The financial appraisal is usually prepared by the quantity surveyor. The QS is the expert on costs and can call on an RICS or other information service, as well as his own knowledge and expertise. Such an appraisal could be a document to be developed as the design progresses, and form a basis for effective cost planning.

However, on a small project where no QS is appointed the architect may have to write an appraisal for inclusion in the feasibility report. This is likely to be little more than an estimate to test the viability of the client's budget figure. A proper cost plan will need to be developed later.

Where the architect undertakes to prepare this appraisal, the approach should be as follows.

Define status

Define the status of the appraisal, and set out the assumptions on which estimates are made. List any items of important information which were not available, and which items have not been included for.

State basis for estimates

State the basis for estimates (eg cost indices, £ per m^2 etc) on current or predicted rates (if projected, to what date).

Estimate capital cost

When estimating the capital cost of the building project, consider:
- location (eg whether remote) and access (eg a difficult tight site);
- site investigation and abnormal site works;
- demolition or preliminary contracts for enabling works;
- programme and phasing;
- building substructure and superstructure (eg systems, cladding etc);
- finishes (eg expensive or standard);
- engineering services installations;
- designers and contractors contingencies;
- fitting out and furnishings;
- landscape treatment both hard and soft, including planting.

Other costs

Other costs to be taken into account might include:
- fees for statutory approvals;
- fees and expenses for the design team;
- fees and expenses for the Planning Supervisor.

An estimate should also clarify the VAT position, the possible effects of inflation, and warn that fluctuations are possible after the start of the building contract, even a lump sum contract. It might also be helpful to suggest the phasing of payments so that the client can begin to consider how best to manage his cash flow.

In addition to the estimate of the capital cost of the building project, the client will need to take into account the cost of the site, legal and other fees, finance costs, the risk and profit element, and an assessment of costs in use for the building.

Outline proposals C

C/1   **Activities**

C/2   **Actions**

C/3   **Stage summary**

C/4   **Watchpoints**

C/5   **Action checks**

Supplement

C/S1   Design and build documentation

C/S2   Design brief: checklist

C/S3   Design team roles

Description

With a traditional procurement method, at Stage C a design concept based on feasibility studies, or a study commissioned by the client from others, will usually be prepared. This will show the design analysis and options considered, and be sufficiently detailed to establish in broad terms the outline proposal preferred. Presentation will normally entail drawings and a report, although more sophisticated techniques such as video or CD-ROM may be employed where appropriate.

Where there is no outline design concept, for example when conserving a historic building, then Stage C will involve the presentation of outline proposals appropriate to the commission.

With design and build, the Employer's Requirements are likely to feature prominently at Stage C. An outline design will probably form part of the Requirements, and this will be taken to an extent related to the intended design contribution by the contractor. With a Contractor Client, the Employer's Requirements received will be regarded as a brief to which the Contractor's Proposals will form a response. Tendering is often a two stage process, and this might initially require outline design only, with design development left until a later stage.

Terminology

  * The RIBA Plan of Work refers to Stage C as Outline Proposals.

  * RIBA standard appointing documents generally refer to Stage C as Outline Proposals.

  * The same terminology is used where the commission relates to work on Historic Buildings. With Community Architecture projects the scope of Stage C might be extended to include additional User Client meetings and information specifically for lay communication.

  * Services for design and build with an Employer Client generally refer to Stage C as Employer's Requirements: Outline Proposals. With a Contractor Client, Stage C services will relate to Contractor's Proposals.

If coming new to the project at this Stage in the Plan of Work, carry out the relevant Pre-Agreement checks and note any General Procedures listed under earlier Stages which might apply.

If taking over a project on which others were engaged for earlier Plan of Work Stages, allow for familiarisation and checking of all usable material when agreeing fees and timetable with the client.

General procedures

. Establish the scope and content of Stage C. Put it into context particularly if it follows Stages undertaken by others, or material produced is likely to be acted upon by others taking over subsequent Stages.

. Agree with the client the extent of professional services for Stage C if not yet settled, and confirm in writing.

. Agree with the client the methods and levels of charging for Stage C if not yet settled, and confirm in writing.

. Assess office resources needed for Stage C and ensure that they are adequate and available.

. Review the project quality plan, update and develop it as necessary.

. Check progress against the timetable for services regularly.

. Check expenditure against the office job cost allocation for Stage C.

. Report regularly to the client on fees and expenses incurred, and submit accounts at agreed intervals.

. Check that the client settles all accounts promptly.

. Check whether the client has confirmed in writing acceptance of Stage A–B proposals or recommendations submitted. Review client's comments on these and decide what action is necessary.

. Check whether the Project Brief for Stage C still meets the client's requirements set out initially, and that any subsequent changes have been authorised by the client.

Preliminary issues

Concerning the client

. Check that the brief as presently developed still meets the client's requirements, budget and timetable. Any amendments should be agreed with the client and confirmed in writing.

. Check whether the client has confirmed in writing acceptance of the feasibility proposals submitted at Stage A–B. There may still be points to discuss and develop during Stage C.

. Make specific requests to the client for further necessary information if that provided is not adequate.

· Alert the client to any matters raised during preliminary discussions with statutory or other bodies which seem likely to affect the brief or design proposals.

· Advise the client on the need to appoint further consultants and specialists. Design decisions may be needed for Outline Proposals which require specialist advice on structure, services and environmental matters.

· Remind the client about the need to appoint a Planning Supervisor early to coordinate matters connected with the pre-tender Health and Safety Plan at this design stage.

Design and build

· Confirm with the client the extent of information to be included in the Employer's Requirements. *(Employer Client)*

· Check the Employer's Requirements issued for tendering purposes, and advise the client on any apparent omissions or inconsistencies. Confirm with the client the extent of information to be provided for inclusion in the Contractor's Proposals. *(Contractor Client)*

Concerning other bodies

· Hold further discussions as appropriate with the Planning Officer to determine whether planning permission is required and if so the procedures and forms to be used. Enquire, where appropriate, whether the planning authority statutory lists and statutory registers are readily available for inspection.

· Enquire from local authority Building Control department whether the project is one which will require approval under Building Regulations. If so, discuss whether this should be Building Notice or Full Plans submission.

· Establish whether it would be more beneficial to submit Building Regulations applications to the local authority or an Approved Inspector, and report to the client.

· Enquire whether a dispensation would be likely where the legal requirements of Building Regulations could be particularly onerous and damaging to the architectural integrity of a historic building.

· Discuss with the relevant authorities the most satisfactory way of making provision for persons with a disability who could be expected to use the building.

· Check Health and Safety legislation requirements likely to affect the planning, circulation, and work station layouts.

· Check whether there is local legislation or legislation particular to the proposed development or building type which should be complied with.

· Check whether bodies such as the National Rivers Authority, British Waterways Board etc could have their interests affected by the proposed development. If this seems possible, they should be consulted.

Preliminary issues
continued

- Check with relevant authorities concerning highways, drainage, water, gas and electricity etc and note requirements for plant and meter housings, substations etc.

Team working

- Check scope of professional services agreed with design team members as they are appointed.

- Confirm agreed common policy towards matters of accountability, warranties, professional indemnity insurance etc.

- Appraise the client's comments on Stage A–B proposals and decide appropriate action.

- Check Design Brief and confirm any changes from the Project Brief.

- Confirm stage timetable for services.

- Confirm programme and pattern for design team meetings.

Costs

- Obtain cost appraisal for Stage C proposals from QS and compare with the client's budget figures or as amended. Report to the client.

- Obtain cost plan from QS and discuss the cost implications of design decisions before they are taken.

Design and build

- Provide information to contractor's estimators for costing out design proposals. *(Contractor Client)*

- Continue resource control procedures for office, and monitor expenditure against allocation of fee for the Stage.

- Report to the client on cost matters at agreed intervals.

Approvals/consents

Hold informal discussions with authorities as appropriate before making formal submission for permission, approval or consent.

- Prepare application for Outline Planning Permission if not yet obtained, and submit application if instructed by client.

- Submit applications for necessary approvals or consents required from third parties if instructed by the client.

Inspections/tests

· Make further visits to the site and/or existing buildings as necessary.

· Advise the client on the need to authorise further survey work if appropriate.

· Construct contour or block models as appropriate to demonstrate options in Outline Proposals.

· Use computer programmes to test and demonstrate environmental impact.

Contract

· Obtain preliminary information from specialist subcontractors and suppliers as necessary for outline design.

Stage input

Information necessary during Stage C might include the following as relevant:

- Brief developed to Project Brief stage.

- Stage A–B proposals as accepted by the client with written confirmation, incorporating any agreed amendments.

- Further information as requested, supplied by client.

- Cost appraisal for Stage A–B prepared by quantity surveyor.

- Notes, sketches, details made on further visits to site and/or existing buildings.

- Published material, technical press articles as appropriate.

- Technical information (eg Planning or Design Guides, British Standards, Codes of Practice etc). Manufacturers' trade literature.

- Results of surveys and tests conducted during Stage A–B.

- Relevant legislation, Circulars or Guides to assist in statutory compliance.

- Contributions, information and recommendations from consultants and specialists.

Design and build

- Employer's Requirements as issued to tenderers. *(Contractor Client)*

Stage output

Tangible results/material produced before the conclusion of Stage C might include the following as relevant:

- Design Brief developed from the Project Brief.

- Outline Proposals. These might show diagrammatic analysis of requirements, use of site, solutions to functional and circulation problems, relationship of spaces, massing, construction and environmental methods.

- A cost appraisal sufficient to allow a cost plan to be prepared (see Fig C.01), and to enable an approximation of construction costs to be made.

- Where appropriate, proposals developed sufficiently to allow an application for Outline Planning Permission.

- Where appropriate, special presentation material.

Design and build

- Outline proposals for Employer's Requirements. *(Employer Client)*

- Outline drawings for Contractor's Proposals. *(Contractor Client)*

- Notes, sketches, details, to facilitate written material and estimates in connection with Contractor's Proposals. *(Contractor Client)*

Fig C.01   Specimen cost plan/budget estimate

Job no: Job title:

Cost plan / budget estimate

		Cost of element	Cost per m² gross floor area	Element shown as % of whole
Substructure		_____	_____	_____
Superstructure	Frame	_____	_____	_____
	Upper floors	_____	_____	_____
	Roof	_____	_____	_____
	Stairs	_____	_____	_____
	External cladding	_____	_____	_____
	Windows and external doors	_____	_____	_____
	Internal partitions	_____	_____	_____
	Internal doors and windows	_____	_____	_____
Internal finishes	Ceiling finishes	_____	_____	_____
	Wall finishes	_____	_____	_____
	Floor finishes	_____	_____	_____
Fittings	Furniture and fittings	_____	_____	_____
Services	Sanitary installation	_____	_____	_____
	Mechanical installation	_____	_____	_____
	Electrical installation	_____	_____	_____
	Special installations	_____	_____	_____
	Elevators and hoists	_____	_____	_____
	Builder's work	_____	_____	_____
	Builder's profit and attendance	_____	_____	_____
Building work	**Sub-total**	_____	_____	_____
Additional	Site works	_____	_____	_____
	Drainage	_____	_____	_____
	External services	_____	_____	_____
	Extra temporary works (phasing)	_____	_____	_____
	Inflation at 3%	_____	_____	_____
	Preliminaries at 5%	_____	_____	_____
Total	**Excluding VAT and contingencies**	_____	_____	_____

* As the brief develops to a Design Brief, continue to develop and authenticate the basis of information. Do not rely on assumptions.

* Consultants should play an increasing part in the development of the brief and the design concept. Keep them involved in the discussions.

* If there are changes to the brief or design as approved, make sure that these are subject to the control procedures already established.

* Remind all consultants and specialists contributing at Stage C of the current legislation (eg building regulations, health and safety) with which the project must conform.

* Cooperate with the Planning Supervisor and all other designers over carrying out risk assessments and in drafting the pre-tender Health and Safety Plan.

* Make sure that structural and services consultants design to meet performance standards, environmental provisions and budget allocation, and present material in a way which can be readily integrated into the overall design concept.

* Innovation in design, specification, or selection of materials and methods can involve risk. Take care that risks are assessed before proposals are finalised. Check and test against known criteria – do not trust to luck.

* Check the extent of existing buildings, site boundaries etc before completing outline design or proposals. In the case of design and build particularly, the Employer normally carries total responsibility for accuracy.

* Watch the budget figure, and monitor the cost of design decisions with the QS. This applies particularly where services systems are a significant proportion of the total building costs or where the design has some unusual features.

* Keep careful records of all conversations, consultations and design team meetings. File notes and sketches prepared during the outline design process. Keep all manufacturers' or trade literature to which reference was made. It might be needed later as proof of the 'state of the art' at the time.

* Think the proposals through before making the presentation. Do not allow yourself to be pressured into accepting unrealistic timescales.

		Tick if relevant	Initial if completed
01	Establish scope, content and context for Stage activities		
02	Check client's written instruction to proceed		
03	If coming new to project, refer to previous Stage checks		
04	Check appointing documents wrt services and fees		
05	Check client has settled all accounts submitted to date		
06	Review and develop project quality plan as necessary		
07	Check office resources wrt services, timetable, fee		
08	Review with design team client's response to Stage AB proposals		
09	Review with team client's response to Project Brief, record changes		
10	Advise client on need for further consultants, specialists		
11	Review consultants' etc services, timetable etc		
12	Obtain relevant technical information and trade literature		
13	Make further site/building visits as authorised		
14	Prepare models for testing, record and analyse results		
15	Advise client on H & S, appointment of Planning Supervisor (P/S)		
16	Discuss further with client procurement options, implications		
17	Obtain project-specific information from S/Cs, suppliers		
18	Discuss with client arrangements for S/Cs and supply tenders		
19	Advise client on arrangements for advance orders		
20	Advise client on contract for preliminary/enabling works		
21	Check with PI insurers if proposals are innovative		
22	Hold informal meetings with statutory bodies, if advisable		
23	Consult user clients/third parties, adjoining owners, if authorised		
24	Monitor office expenditure against fee income		
25	Develop Project Brief into Design Brief		
26	Collate information from QS, other consultants and specialists		
27	Prepare outline planning permission if instructed		
28	Prepare Outline Proposals and Report and submit to client		
29			
30			

Supplement

C

C/S1   **Design and build documentation**

C/S2   **Design brief: checklist**

C/S3   **Design team roles**

Design and build documentation

Employer's Requirements

The amount of information to be included in the Employer's Requirements can vary enormously. A straightforward project requiring a relatively simple design solution which can be left largely to the contractor may need little more than basic details of site and accommodation. With a more complex problem, or a design which needs sensitivity of detail, the Employer's Requirements might extend to a full scheme design.

The number and detail of documents which make up the Employer's Requirements will be influenced by considerations such as:
- how much design control the Employer wishes to retain, for example in the interests of maintenance programmes or because of functional requirements;
- whether the Employer regards the process as more of a develop and construct operation, where only constructional details are left in the hands of the contractor;
- whether contractor's standard unit types will form the basis of the scheme;
- whether the Employer will require design continuity via novation or a 'consultant switch';
- whether the Employer has appointed a Planning Supervisor and a pre-tender Health and Safety Plan exists.

Generally the Requirements will always need to include basic information, such as the following.
- Site information and requirements (eg boundaries, topography, known subsoil conditions).
- Site constraints (eg limitations of access, storage) and relevant easements or restrictive covenants.
- Planning permission obtained or conditions known (contractors will not usually tender until outline planning permission has been obtained).
- Functional nature of the building(s) (eg kind and number of units) and accommodation requirements.
- Schematic layout of the building (or more developed design as appropriate).
- Specific requirements as to forms of construction, materials, services, finishes, equipment etc.
- Details of special programming requirements (eg phased completion).
- Contract data or special requirements (eg named subcontractors, as built information).
- Requirements concerning contractor's design liability, insurance cover, design team, requirement to use Employer's designers etc.
- Clear statement of the extent of information and detail to be included in the Contractor's Proposals.
- Content and form of the Contract Sum Analysis.

It is generally accepted that too specific an approach over design and constructional matters, or the specifying of proprietary systems and materials, may reduce the contractor's design liability in the event of a failure.

Contractor's Proposals

These will be in direct response to the Employer's Requirements. Architects acting as consultants to a Contractor Client will first need to check the information provided to establish whether it is adequate. A query list is often necessary to obtain clarification on matters of conflict or omission.

Submissions sometimes take the form of an A3 brochure, and typically include for the following.
- Design drawings (eg site layout, floor plans, elevations, principal sections, some detailed drawings, landscaping).
- Structural details (eg foundation and structure – general arrangement drawings).
- Mechanical services (eg layouts of ducts, pipe runs, schematic indications for all systems).
- Electrical services (eg floor layouts showing lighting, power, alarms).
- Specifications (eg particular for trades – prescription and performance; general specification for workmanship, materials, finishes).
- Programme (eg bar chart).
- Method statements (eg general organisational matters and in particular Health and Safety Plan proposals).

The tender figure will usually be required to be made separately. With it will be the Contract Sum Analysis.

The structure of the Contract Sum Analysis will be in accordance with the Employer's Requirements. A typical breakdown could be:
- Design work
- Preliminaries
- Health and safety provisions
- Demolition
- Excavation
- Concrete
- Brickwork and blockwork
- Roofing and cladding
- Woodwork
- Structural steelwork
- Metalwork
- Mechanical and plumbing services
- Electrical services
- Glazing
- Painting and decorating
- Drainage and external works.

Architects involved with design and build should take note of information contained in:
- JCT Practice Notes CD/1A and CD/1B
- NJCC Code of Procedure for Selective Tendering for Design and Build.

Design brief: checklist

The Design Brief relevant at the end of Stage C is developed from the Project Brief, and will include amendments instructed by the client and agreed with the design team. All changes to the Project Brief will be subject to the control procedures set down in the Project Quality Plan.

The brief is developed to include further or updated information as follows:

Functional

- schedule of functions or processes, activities, spatial relationships, installations (see Fig C.02)
- organisational structure of operations.

Design objectives

- accommodation requirements
- space standards
- environmental standards
- environmental performance requirements
- image and quality
- flexibility to accommodate future reorganisation
- allowance for future expansion or extension
- life span for structure, elements, installations
- operational and maintenance requirements
- special considerations (eg security).

Design constraints

- site constraints (physical and legal)
- legislative constraints
- programme constraints
- cost constraints.

Fig C.02   Specimen schedule of activities/spaces/rooms

Job no: Job title:

Schedule of activities/spaces/rooms

Activities/spaces/ rooms identified	Preferred aspect and location	Functional connections	Notes of specific requirements
Compiled by:			Date

Quantity surveyor

The QS can assist the design team in reviewing financial aspects of the outline proposals, and monitoring costs against the budget. He should be involved continuously and report regularly at design team meetings.

The QS will prepare the master cost plan, relying on input from other design team members.

Structural engineer

The engineer can work with the architect to develop structural concepts which are integral with the overall design. He should also liaise with services engineers to ensure integrated design. Priorities should be established and conflicts resolved at design team meetings.

Building services engineers

At outline proposals stage, the architect will take into account orientation, climatic and other environmental factors. There will also be a need to establish performance, installation costs and costs in use. The services consultants can play an important role in contributing to an integrated design approach. They should contribute regularly to design team meetings.

> **Health and safety**
>
> All design team members should cooperate with the Planning Supervisor in carrying out risk assessments, and starting to prepare material for inclusion in the Health and Safety File and the pre-tender Health and Safety Plan.

Scheme Design D

D/1   **Activities**

D/2   **Actions**

D/3   **Stage summary**

D/4   **Watchpoints**

D/5   **Action checks**

Supplement

D/S1   Scheme design presentation

D/S2   Design team roles

Description

At Stage D, under traditional procurement, the outline proposals approved by the client are taken to a more detailed level, or, in the case of design, to a full design scheme. Fig D.01 illustrates the process of design development. As lead consultant the architect will need to be satisfied that there are no insurmountable problems ahead concerning the integration of consultants' proposals into the overall design concept. As 'designer', within the meaning of that term in the CDM Regulations, the architect will also have to be sure that all health and safety implications have been properly considered at this stage.

With design and build, where the architect is acting for an Employer Client, Stage D might cover only the start of design formulation to the extent necessary for inclusion as part of the Employer's Requirements. With a Contractor Client, development of the design information included as part of the Contractor's Proposals will probably not take place until there is confirmation that the contractor's bid has been approved, or a second stage tender is invited.

Where management procurement is followed, there will still need to be an overall design scheme pending 'Project Drawings'. It might be necessary to give consideration to the breakdown into works packages during this design stage, and this in turn might influence some design decisions.

Terminology

* The RIBA Plan of Work refers to Stage D as Scheme Design.

* RIBA standard appointing documents generally refer to Stage D as Scheme Design.

* Different terminology is sometimes used where the commission relates to work on Historic Buildings, where Stage D refers to Detailed Proposals and Statutory Consents.

* In design and build with an Employer Client, Stages D–G are often grouped as 'Employer's Requirements'. With a Contractor Client, Stage H usually precedes Stages D–E, which are often termed Design Development.

Fig D.01   **The process of brief and design development**

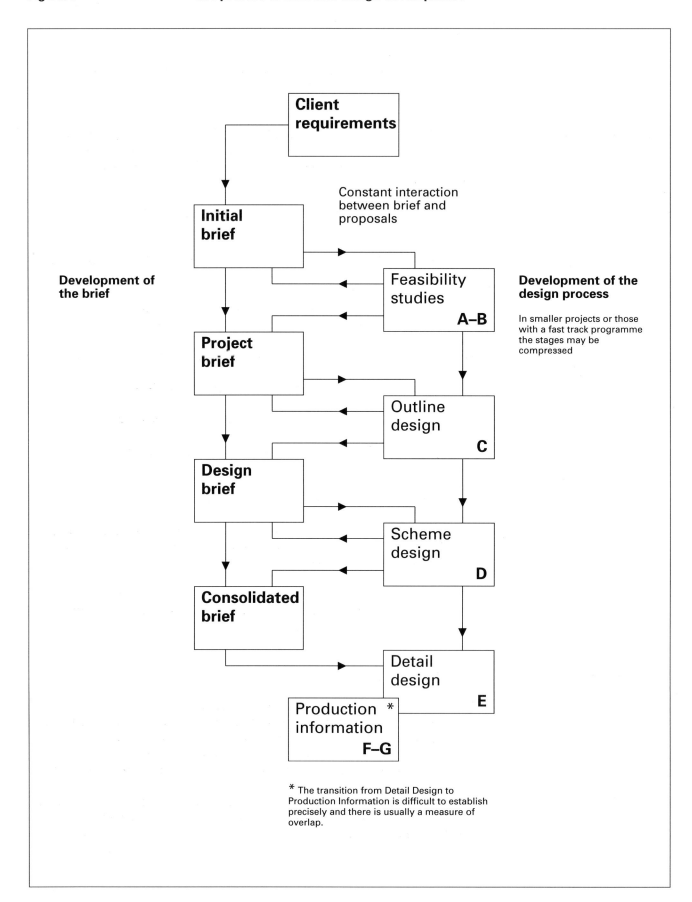

Client requirements

Constant interaction between brief and proposals

Initial brief

Development of the brief

Feasibility studies

A–B

Project brief

Development of the design process

In smaller projects or those with a fast track programme the stages may be compressed

Outline design

C

Design brief

Scheme design

D

Consolidated brief

Detail design

E

Production information *

F–G

* The transition from Detail Design to Production Information is difficult to establish precisely and there is usually a measure of overlap.

If coming new to the project at this Stage in the Plan of Work, carry out the relevant Pre-Agreement checks and note any General Procedures listed under earlier Stages which might apply.

If taking over a project on which others were engaged for earlier Plan of Work Stages, allow for familiarisation and checking of all usable material when agreeing fees and timetable with the client.

General procedures

- Establish the scope and content of Stage D. Put it into context, particularly if it follows Stages undertaken by others. If possible establish whether material produced now is likely to be acted upon by others taking over subsequent Stages.

- Agree with the client the extent of professional services for Stage D if not yet settled, and confirm in writing.

- Agree with the client the methods and levels of charging for Stage D if not yet settled, and confirm in writing.

- Assess office resources needed for Stage D and ensure that they are adequate and available.

- Review the project quality plan, update and develop it as necessary.

- Check progress against the timetable for services regularly.

- Check expenditure against the office job cost allocation for Stage D.

- Report regularly to the client on fees and expenses incurred, and submit accounts at agreed intervals.

- Check that the client settles all accounts promptly.

- Check whether the client has confirmed in writing acceptance of Stage C outline proposals as submitted. Review client's comments on these and decide what action is necessary.

- Check whether the Design Brief for Stage D still meets the client's requirements set out initially, and that any subsequent changes have been authorised by the client and dealt with by the control procedures.

Preliminary issues

Concerning the client

- Check that the brief as presently developed still meets the client's requirements, budget and timetable. Any amendments should be agreed with the client and confirmed in writing. Advise the client that a Consolidated Brief will be formulated during Stage D and warn that any modifications thereafter could mean abortive work and additional expense.

- Check whether the client has confirmed in writing acceptance of the outline proposals submitted at Stage C. There may be points to discuss and develop during Stage D.

Preliminary issues
continued

- Advise the client about any proposals to introduce innovative design or construction ideas or the specifying of relatively new materials, and ask the client to confirm awareness of these in writing.

- Advise the client on the need to appoint further consultants and specialists.

- Alert the client about any matters raised during discussions with statutory or other bodies which might affect the proposals. Explain the implications and discuss what action should be taken.

- Check that all information requested from the client concerning the site or existing buildings has been supplied and verified.

- Ask the client for information and requirements concerning processes, plant and other installations, room layouts and equipment etc and record this information appropriately (see Fig D.02). Check on particular requirements concerning the life expectancy of components, fittings and installations, and performance requirements for environmental and services aspects etc.

- Alert the client to the design implications arising out of Health and Safety legislation (eg circulation, design of work stations, environmental comfort etc) and implications for future maintenance, repair and replacement.

- Check whether the client wishes the project to be planned to allow for phasing of completion or completion to a particular sequence. This might have design implications.

- Check whether the client has decided the method of procurement. This decision could affect the amount and type of design information needed at this Stage.

Concerning other bodies

- Discuss with the Planning Officer any difficulties or conditions arising from an Outline Planning Permission, and any problems likely with a Full Planning application. Check whether the authority operates particular planning policies, issues its own supplementary guidance notes etc.

- Discover whether the planning authority requires information additional to that on the usual form of application for Full Planning Permission, and whether additional copies could speed up the consultation process.

- Enquire whether representation at planning committee when the application is considered is possible, should this be thought desirable.

- Continue discussions with Building Control and the Fire authorities over matters where overall design could be fundamentally affected, eg compartmentation, atrium design, escape routes, smoke lobbies etc.

- Check Health and Safety legislation requirements likely to affect detail planning. Continue to cooperate with the Planning Supervisor and other designers over design implications of the pre-tender Health and Safety Plan required under the CDM Regulations.

- Continue checks with relevant authorities for highways, drainage, water, gas, electricity supplies etc.

Fig D.02 **Specimen room data notes sheet**

Job no: Job title:

Room data notes

Room reference

Function/
functional requirements

User requirements

Relationships and
connections

Critical dimensions

Layout and flexibility

Floor loadings

Technical performance
standards

Lighting

Power

Heating/ventilation

Engineering installations

Finishes

Fittings

Other particular
requirements

Compiled by: Date

Preliminary issues
continued

Team working

- Check scope of professional services agreed with additional design team members or specialists as they are appointed.

- Appraise the client's comments on Stage C Outline Proposals and decide appropriate action.

- Check the Consolidated Brief and confirm any changes from the Design Brief.

- Appraise input from specialist firms, including potential subcontractors and suppliers.

- Integrate and coordinate input from design team members and specialists.

- Confirm Stage timetable for services.

- Confirm programme and pattern for design team meetings.

Costs

- Prepare cost appraisal for Stage D Scheme Design and compare with the client's original budget figures or as amended. Report to the client.

- Review cost plan and monitor cost implications of design decisions.

Design and build

- Provide information to other consultants and contractor's estimators to cost scheme design proposals. *(Contractor Client)*

- Continue resource control procedures for office, and monitor expenditure against allocation of fee for Stage.

- Report to the client on cost matters at agreed intervals.

Approvals/consents

- Continue discussions as appropriate before making a formal submission for permission, approval or consent.

- Prepare application for Approval of Reserved Matters following an Outline Planning Permission if appropriate.

- Prepare application for Full Planning Permission, Listed Building Consent, Conservation Area Consent as relevant.

- Prepare application for Express Consent to Display an Advertisement, application or notification to fell or lop trees covered by a Tree Preservation Order or in a Conservation Area, as relevant.

- Prepare design information as required by Planning Supervisor for incorporation into the pre-tender Health and Safety Plan and submit for comment.

- Submit planning applications if instructed by client, and accompanied by relevant documents including cheque from client for the appropriate fee.

Inspections/tests

- Arrange to inspect similar projects elsewhere if appropriate, perhaps accompanied by the client. Appraise and analyse the schemes. It would be wise to check first that expenditure is authorised by the client.

- Conduct or arrange for tests to be conducted using physical or computer models as appropriate (eg in research laboratory using wind tunnel, heliodon, artificial sky etc) to obtain and analyse information about environmental performance, air circulation, temperature distribution etc.

- Conduct or arrange for relevant tests to be conducted on structural performance, durability, consistency etc of components, fittings and finishes.

- Arrange for production prototypes, mock-ups, sample components and panels to be tested under specified conditions and to stipulated methods as appropriate.

Contract

- Confirm with the client the procurement method to be adopted.

- Confirm with the client the type of contract to be used.

- Consider preliminary tender action for specialist subcontractors and suppliers.

- Discuss with the client particular requirements for phased or sectional completion.

D/3 Stage summary

Stage input

Information necessary during Stage D might include the following as relevant:

- Brief developed to Design Brief stage.

- Stage C proposals as accepted by the client in written confirmation, incorporating any agreed design changes.

- Further information as requested by the architect and supplied by the client.

- Notes, sketches, details made on visits to other projects.

- Relevant published material, technical information etc.

- Results of tests conducted during Stage C.

- Relevant legislation, Circulars or Guides.

- Further contributions, information and recommendations from consultants and specialists.

- Cost appraisal for Stage C prepared by quantity surveyor.

Stage output

Tangible results/material produced before the conclusion of Stage D might include the following as relevant:

- Consolidated Brief developed from the Design Brief.

- Scheme design showing coordinated design intentions, site layout, planning and spatial arrangements, elevational treatment, construction and environmental systems and buildability.

- Developed proposals for existing, perhaps historic, buildings, with information from conservators and other consultants.

- A cost appraisal including an estimate of construction costs.

- Prototypes, mock-ups, models, sample panels etc.

- Proposals developed sufficiently to allow an application for Full Planning Permission/Listed Building Consent/Conservation Area Consent etc as applicable.

Design and build

- Scheme design for incorporation into Employer's Requirements (part of Stages D–G). *(Employer Client)*

- Further notes, sketches, details and drawings as necessary to develop the scheme included in the Contractor's Proposals (part of Stages D–E). *(Contractor Client)*

*   Maintain close collaboration with consultants and specialists. The architect might not be responsible for their individual performances, but will be responsible for the coordination and integration of their work into the overall design.

*   As lead consultant or design team leader, the architect has an obligation to check that every designer pays regard to the CDM Regulations and avoids foreseeable risks, or takes steps to combat them at source when designing.

*   When designing to meet legislative standards or codes of practice, check that these are the current versions.

*   When adopting proprietary systems or components for a design, take care that proposals will satisfy British Standards or other technical standards prescribed. Manufacturers tend to overstate product performance in trade literature, and test results, as published, might relate to tests carried out under circumstances quite unlike those which might apply to a particular project. Check that products specified are suitable for the purpose and location, and obtain verification, certificates, warranties as appropriate before making a design commitment.

*   During this stage it is wise to draft preliminary specification notes, and to collate information as it comes to hand. Specification writing is part of the design process, and should be undertaken by the designer.

*   The QS should have a full cost plan prepared at Stage D, and there must be regular two-way exchange of information if designers are to keep within cost targets or limits.

*   When producing a scheme design it will be necessary to make regular checks against the brief as last updated. It is all too easy to overlook small but crucial requirements in the excitement of designing.

*   The presentation to the client of Stage D proposals is particularly important. Establish early how this is to be effected, and prepare the material accordingly. It will usually entail a written report and visual material. It may require an oral presentation.

*   At the conclusion of Stage D, get the satisfied client to 'sign off' the Scheme Design and the Consolidated Brief. Clearly, beyond this point any changes which are client-originated might mean abortive work and additional expense.

*   When preparing the submission and presentation of the Scheme Design, do not overlook the client's stipulations, costs, transmission arrangements. Take nothing for granted – so much depends on successful communication.

D/5   Action checks

		Tick if relevant	Initial if completed
01	Establish scope, content and context for Stage activities		
02	Check client's written instruction to proceed		
03	If coming new to project, refer to previous Stage checks		
04	Check appointing documents wrt services and fees		
05	Check client has settled all accounts submitted to date		
06	Review and develop project quality plan as necessary		
07	Check office resources wrt services, timetable, fee		
08	Review with design team client's response to Stage C proposals		
09	Review with team client's response to Design Brief, record changes		
10	Review with consultants' etc services, timetable etc		
11	Obtain Codes, Standards, Digests etc relevant to project		
12	Make further site/building visits as authorised		
13	Prepare models for testing, record and analyse results		
14	Obtain project-specific information from S/Cs, suppliers		
15	Check designers' cooperation with P/S wrt Plan and File		
16	Discuss further with client procurement method, building contract		
17	Consider action on S/Cs and supply tenders		
18	Consider action on advance orders		
19	Hold further meetings with statutory bodies as necessary		
20	Consult user clients/third parties, if authorised		
21	Check that necessary third party consents are obtained		
22	Identify works packages where applicable		
23	Identify performance specified work, contractor's designed portion		
24	Review cost plan and implications of design decisions		
25	Monitor office expenditure against fee income		
26	Develop Design Brief into Consolidated Brief		
27	Collate information from QS, other consultants and specialists		
28	Prepare full planning permission if instructed		
29	Prepare Scheme Design, with presentation material, for client		
30			

Supplement

D

D/S1   **Scheme design presentation**

D/S2   **Design team roles**

D/S1   Scheme design presentation

Scheme presentation to the client at Stage D will be in the most appropriate form, or may have to be in a form directed by the client. A decision should be made as early as possible, and might be influenced by context.

The medium of presentation

Decide how presentation of the scheme design is to be made, eg by:
- the architect in person;
- written report and drawings;
- electronic means at long range (eg software, CD-ROM etc).

The intended recipients

Establish who is to be the immediate recipient of the scheme design presentation (eg client in person or client body committee) and whether the same material will also have a secondary presentation (eg to Planning Committee, public meetings, user client groups).

The end users

Establish the use to which presentation material is likely to be put initially and in the longer term (eg for public display, fund raising, media coverage). This might require production of specially commissioned particular material, or simply multiple copies of the original material being available.

The content

The content of information to be presented, and the media to be used might include, for example:

Written report
- presenting facts for information;
- suggesting and comparing solutions;
- making recommendations;
- including or accompanied by illustrations, drawings and a financial report.

Drawings
- orthographic plans at all levels;
- elevations and cross-sections;
- perspectives etc to give a realistic view of the building exterior;
- computer-generated visual images or analytical diagrams.

Models
- block model (working tool);
- presentation model to show architectural quality, form and colour, landscape setting etc;
- detail model of building part or particular feature etc;
- interior arrangement model to show spaces, arrangements, furniture layouts etc;
- computer-generated models.

Multi-media
- Computer software, video, CD-ROM.

The scheme design presentation will also be influenced by factors such as:
- whether material is to be produced in-house or by outside professionals;
- whether the presentation is covered by a budget allocation, or is to be paid for direct by the client;
- the anticipated life of the material and its subsequent storage;
- costs associated with circulation, transport (particularly if overseas), insurance etc.

Quantity surveyor

The QS should collaborate with the architect and other consultants to develop and refine the full cost plan as the design is developed and outline specification notes are prepared.

The QS should contribute information and advice for inclusion in the Stage D report to the client.

Structural engineer

The structural engineer should collaborate in developing the design and advise on structural options and preferred solutions. The architect is responsible for coordination and integration into the overall design concept. This will include checking that structural proposals are compatible with the space and access requirements of the services installations.

The structural engineer should produce the initial structural design, prescribe profiles, basic specifications, building tolerances, and define basic rules for voids and holes which might need to be provided and which might affect the structure.

The structural engineer should contribute information and advice for inclusion in the Stage D report to the client.

Building services engineer

The services engineers should have developed proposals sufficiently to establish performance specifications to ensure satisfactory integration of services into the overall design scheme. This will mean working within the constraints set by the architect as lead consultant and the structural engineer. Decisions will need to be made on the services layouts and their coordination in relation to the building structure generally; ceiling, floor and wall layouts; and providing satisfactory access for commissioning.

The engineers should liaise closely with the architect on all services aspects, including the location and installation of equipment and plant, services voids, building tolerances, and access for maintenance and repairs.

The building services engineers should contribute information and advice for inclusion in the Stage D report to the client.

Health and safety

All design team members should continue to cooperate with the Planning Supervisor in the preparation of material for inclusion in the Health and Safety File and the pre-tender Health and Safety Plan.

Detail Design

E/1   **Activities**

E/2   **Actions**

E/3   **Stage summary**

E/4   **Watchpoints**

E/5   **Action checks**

Supplement

E/S1   Design information: Implications of procurement method

E/S2   Procedures for the issue of drawings

E/S3   Design team roles

Description

At Stage E under traditional procurement, the approved Scheme Design is worked through in detail. This will extend to matters of construction, choice of materials and standards of workmanship required. There is an imprecise boundary between design information and production information. Consultation with the client and approvals by him will be needed throughout the process, although there will normally be no formal presentation. The client may be expected to contribute information or comments on finishes, furnishings and equipment. Design work by consultants and specialists must be coordinated, and relevant information passed to the Planning Supervisor for inclusion in the Health and Safety Plan or File. Cost checks are essential at this stage to ensure that the design development does not exceed budgetary limits or depart from the requirements of the consolidated brief.

In design and build procurement with an Employer Client, detail design will be taken to the extent agreed. It is relatively rare for the Employer Client to require the Scheme Design to be worked through in detail as part of the Employer's Requirements, and indeed this can be regarded as an abuse of the design build concept. However, some exploratory detail design is often necessary before the Employer's Requirements can be finished.

With a Contractor Client, detail design will usually closely overlap production information. Here the information will normally be domestic in the sense that it will be associated with the work of other consultants to the Contractor, specialist subcontractors and the estimators within the contractor organisation.

With the management procurement approach, detail design is more difficult to resolve. A predetermined amount will rely on the specialists involved with the works packages, and their contributions are unlikely to be available at this stage. Nevertheless, close attention should be given to the appropriate number of packages and control maintained to minimise the risk of overlap or duplication. Detail design with this method cannot be equated with traditional procurement, and much must remain to be resolved after the contract has been let. Great reliance has to be placed on the management contractor or construction manager. Monitoring of detail design will continue well into the construction phase, and the Health and Safety Plan might require regular adjustment.

Terminology

* The RIBA Plan of Work refers to Stage E as Detail Design.

* RIBA standard appointing documents generally refer to Stage E as Detail Design.

* With Community Architecture projects, the scope of Stage E might be extended to include additional User Client requirements concerning negotiations, customisation or detailing for self-build operations.

* In Design and Build with an Employer Client, Stage E might be within the stages termed 'Employer's Requirements'. With a Contractor Client, Stage E is part of 'Design Development'.

If coming new to the project at this Stage in the Plan of Work, carry out the relevant Pre-Agreement checks and note any General Procedures listed under earlier Stages which might apply.

If taking over a project on which others were engaged for earlier Plan of Work Stages, allow for familiarisation and checking of all usable material when agreeing fees and timetable with the client.

General procedures

·   Establish the scope and content of Stage E. Put it into context, particularly if it follows Stages undertaken by others, or material produced now is likely to be acted upon by others taking over subsequent Stages.

·   Agree with the client the extent of professional services for Stage E if not yet settled, and confirm in writing.

·   Agree with the client the methods and levels of charging for Stage E if not yet settled, and confirm in writing.

·   Assess office resources needed for Stage E and ensure that they are adequate and available.

·   Review the project quality plan, update and develop it as necessary.

·   Check progress against the timetable for services regularly.

·   Check expenditure against the office job cost allocation for Stage E.

·   Report regularly to the client on fees and expenses incurred, and submit accounts at agreed intervals.

·   Check that the client settles all accounts promptly.

·   Check whether the client has confirmed in writing acceptance of Stage D scheme design as submitted.

·   Review the client's comments on Stage D submission and decide what action is necessary.

·   Check whether the Consolidated Brief for Stage E still meets the client's requirements set out initially, and that any subsequent changes have been authorised by the client. Any changes beyond this point could result in abortive work which should be chargeable.

Design and build

·   Check whether the client has confirmed in writing acceptance of proposals and information supplied so far to form part of the Employer's Requirements. *(Employer Client)*

·   Check whether the client has confirmed in writing acceptance of design proposals to form part of the Contractor's Proposals. *(Contractor Client)*

Preliminary issues

Concerning the client

· Check whether the client has confirmed in writing acceptance of the scheme design submitted at Stage D. There will be points to discuss and develop during Stage E.

· Check that any design changes now instructed are recorded and subject to control procedures which form part of quality management.

Concerning other bodies

· Discuss with the Planning Officer the implications arising from any conditions attached to a Full Planning Permission. If permission was refused, discuss the reasons for the refusal and prepare for the client recommendations as to the best course of action.

· Continue discussions with Building Control and Fire authorities before making formal application for approval under Building Regulations.

· Continue discussions with relevant authorities for highways, drainage, water, gas, electricity supplies etc on matters concerning detail design.

· Consult insurers regarding the application of Codes of Practice relating to standards and finishes in detail design, and their requirements for fire prevention during site operations which might have design implications.

Team working

· Appraise with other design team members the client's comments on Stage D scheme design and decide appropriate action.

· Appraise input from specialist firms, including potential subcontractors and suppliers.

· Integrate and coordinate input from design team members and specialists.

· Confirm Stage timetable for services.

· Confirm programme and pattern for design team meetings.

Costs

· Review cost appraisal for Stage E in the event of cost implications arising out of amendments or detail design decisions.

· Review cost plan and monitor cost implications of detail design decisions.

· Continue resource control procedures for office, and monitor expenditure against allocation of fee for Stage.

· Report to the client on cost matters at agreed intervals.

Design and build
- Provide any further necessary information to the contractor's estimators. *(Contractor Client)*

- Review estimates received from specialist firms either direct or through consultants for inclusion in tender documents or as basis for provisional sums. *(Contractor Client)*

Approvals/consents

- Continue discussions as appropriate before making a formal submission for approval or consent.

- Continue discussions with the Planning Officer in the event of a refusal of planning permission, even though it may be the subject of appeal.

- Check whether minor amendments to the scheme design at this Stage go beyond the scope of the planning permission granted. If so, it may be necessary to deposit amended drawings.

- Prepare Building Notice for submission under the Building Regulations, or prepare application for approval by deposit of Full Plans. Prepare submission to an Approved Inspector for issue of an Initial Notice for acceptance by the local authority, if this is the chosen option.

- Submit application for necessary approval if instructed by the client, together with relevant documents including cheque from the client for the appropriate fee.

- If a refusal is given, advise the client on the appropriate action, ie either seek dispensation on matters not appropriate or too onerous, or prepare documents with amendments for re-submission to local authority, or refer matter for determination by Secretary of State.

Inspections/tests

- Make such visits as necessary to supply sources (eg quarries, brickyards, stoneyards) and manufacturing sources (eg foundries, factories, workshops) before making final design choices.

- Conduct or arrange for further tests to be conducted as necessary on components, panels and finishes.

Contract

- Initiate tender action for quotations from specialist subcontractors and suppliers.

Stage input

Information necessary during Stage E might include the following as relevant:

- Brief developed to Consolidated Brief stage.

- Stage D proposals as accepted by the client in written confirmation, incorporating any agreed amendments.

- Cost appraisal for Stage D prepared by quantity surveyor.

- Published material. Technical information including samples relevant to the project.

- Results of tests conducted during Stage D.

- Relevant legislation.

- Further contributions, information and recommendations from consultants and specialists including possible subcontractors and suppliers.

Stage output

Tangible results/material produced before the conclusion of Stage E might include the following as relevant:

- Detail design drawings. Prepared largely for investigative purposes these will often overlap production information. They can provide opportunities for coordinating structure, services and specialist installations. Internal spaces may be detailed to include fittings, equipment, finishes. Site work, hard and soft landscape, external and internal features and signing may be detailed. Profiles, dimensional coordination and critical tolerances can be confirmed.

- Specification notes (prescriptive and performance) on materials and workmanship, and notes for draft preambles or preliminaries for Bills of Quantities/Specification/Schedules of Work.

- Further detailed information on proposals for existing, perhaps historic, buildings.

Design and build

- Detail design information for incorporation into Employer's Requirements (part of Stage D–G). *(Employer Client)*

- Further design development drawings and design team members' work on scheme submitted in the Contractor's Proposals (part of Stage D–E). *(Contractor Client)*

* This is usually the most important stage in the architect's design work. Stage E often merges into production information or working drawings, particularly with smaller projects.

* The architect needs to bring both design and management skills to Stage E. Collaboration with other design team members and coordination of their contributions is often difficult to achieve in practice.

* There must be an organised flow of information between architect and consultants. This will help to ensure an appropriate fit of elements, and compatibility between specialists' and builders' work.

* Similarly there must be an organised flow of information between architect and QS. The cost plan will need to be reviewed in the light of comments by the client and design decisions.

* Design decisions are made and subsequent design changes should be subject to proper control procedures in accordance with the project quality plan. No design team members should attempt to make decisions unilaterally.

* Services consultants will soon be preparing subcontract tendering documents. To avoid the complication of collateral agreements, design work is best not entrusted to subcontractors unless unavoidable.

* Give the client reasonable notice to supply detailed final requirements concerning access, facilities, furnishings, fittings etc. Likewise take into account the users' requirements as relevant.

* Have an agreed policy for coordinating information on drawings. The use of copy or base negatives is rational, but these must be kept updated.

* Systematically compile and update notes for specification or schedules as further materials are chosen and standards of workmanship set.

* Remember that the procurement method chosen will greatly affect the amount of detail design information necessary at this stage.

* On smaller projects where the architect might also be appointed as Planning Supervisor, this is a good time to check the form and content of the pre-tender Health and Safety Plan.

Action checks

		Tick if relevant	Initial if completed
01	Establish scope, content and context for Stage activities		
02	Check client's written instruction to proceed		
03	If coming new to project, refer to previous Stage checks		
04	Check appointing documents wrt services and fees		
05	Check client has settled all accounts submitted to date		
06	Review and develop project quality plan as necessary		
07	Check office resources wrt services, timetable, fee		
08	Review with design team client's response to Stage D proposals		
09	Review with consultants' etc services, timetable etc		
10	Obtain project-specific information from S/Cs, suppliers		
11	Check designers' cooperation with P/S wrt H & S Plan and File		
12	Obtain samples etc and submit to client for comment		
13	Obtain client's written approval of materials, finishes		
14	Consult user clients/third parties, if authorised		
15	Hold further meetings with statutory bodies (eg Fire, Bldg Control)		
16	Consult insurers on application of LPC Fire Codes etc		
17	Review implications of planning permission conditions		
18	Check adequacy of info. on building services for detail design		
19	Initiate tender action, with documents, for S/Cs, suppliers		
20	Inspect tenders and info. submitted by S/Cs, suppliers		
21	Discuss with client main contract tender list and procedures		
22	Prepare special presentation panels etc for client		
23	Review cost plan and implications of detail design decisions		
24	Monitor office expenditure against fee income		
25	Collate information from QS, other consultants and specialists		
26	Draft preliminary notes for Bills/Spec/Schedules of Work		
27	Prepare Building Notice/Full Plans under Bldg Regs if instructed		
28	Complete Detail Design proposals and report to client		
29			
30			

Supplement

E/S1   **Design information:**
            Implications of procurement method

E/S2   **Procedures for the issue of drawings**

E/S3   **Design team roles**

Design information:
Implications of procurement method

The production of information, its amount, type and timing, is likely to be directly affected by the procurement method chosen and ultimately by the type of contract selected.

This will be manifest at contract stage, and in the documentation prepared for tendering purposes. The desired balance between graphic and written information, between drawings and schedules, or specification notes and bills of quantities, is an important factor in the content and structuring of information. It will also indicate which documents are intended to take precedence in the event of conflict, and therefore which warrant the greatest care and attention in preparation. The extent to which there is to be contractual reliance on drawings might determine their form and detail.

It is important to identify at detail design stage who will have responsibility for producing what information – architect, consultants, or contractor, specialist firms etc.

The more complex the pattern of information required the greater the risk of omissions, errors and inconsistencies between documents. The greater too is the need for collaboration in order to bring about integration and coordination of design information.

Even using best endeavours it is rarely possible to bring a traditional procurement lump sum project to a fully designed state pre-tender. Most building contracts accept the need for further information to be issued during progress of the works.

With design and build, or management contracts, it is recognised that a substantial amount of detail design work will take place after the main contract has been let.

In an attempt to control the amount and flow of information, and recognising that everything will not always be available at the start of a contract, a schedule of information still to be provided is sometimes agreed beforehand by the architect and the contractor.

Sometimes the successful tenderer is required to inspect the documentation and provide the client with verification that it will be sufficient to carry out and complete the project. Then, should it be necessary to produce further drawings or calculations, this will be the contractor's risk. However, the architect will then be involved in checking the contractor's submissions to ensure that detail design is not compromised.

Value Engineering

Value Engineering is a fairly recent innovation in construction projects. In essence it involves bringing in an independent consultant 'value engineer' to explore thoroughly the design proposals for efficiency and cost effectiveness. This can necessitate substantial last minute redesign work. For this reason a full Value Engineering exercise by an independent consultant should not be left later than Stage E, with perhaps a further Value Audit at tender stage. Although in principle applicable to all methods of procurement, Value Engineering is more likely to be of benefit with the larger complex projects usually associated with management procurement.

**Design information
flow**

Traditional procurement

1 Origination
Design information can originate from:
- architect
- design team members
- specialist subcontractors and suppliers
- main contractor (to the extent provided for in the contract).

2 Coordination and integration
Responsibility for coordinating and integrating such information into the overall design rests with the architect as lead consultant, or design team leader.

3 Detail design work
Some detail design work is necessary for all projects and should be started as soon as practicable. The transition from detail design Stage E to production information Stage F is not easily defined. There will inevitably be a measure of overlap which might vary from project to project. With small projects the two stages might be merged.

4 Design development
With traditional procurement where a project is to be fully designed before work on site commences, Stage E provides an opportunity to develop and refine the design intentions. The scheme can be systematically explored and parts expanded to a larger scale in plan, section, or three dimensions. Potentially awkward junctions can be identified and resolved. Zones may be introduced and a grid discipline imposed.

5 Avoidance of conflict and overlap
Design information originating from various sources should be coordinated to eliminate any conflict between structure and services, to make sure that different services are not competing for the same duct spaces, or that holes are not expected at critical structural points. Design integrity and quality should not

Fig E.01

Design information flow: traditional procurement

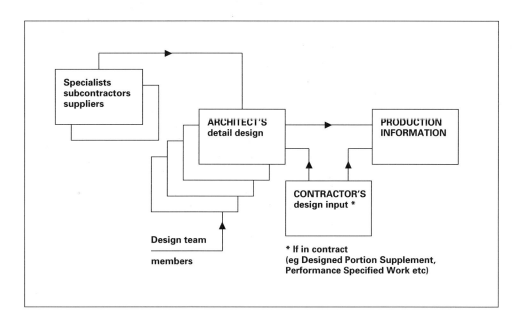

need to be sacrificed because of the requirements of other design team members, but achieving acceptable compromise and satisfactory integration can be a demanding process.

Smaller projects which might need only a dozen or so drawings, and very limited input from consultants, are unlikely to present real problems in terms of integration and coordination.

Larger and more complex projects will need a more formalised set of procedures. The design concept is likely to be founded on a totally integrated approach. There should be an agreed strategy for the coordination of information between the architect and other design team members.

Design information flow

Design and build procurement

1 Origination
Design information can originate from:
· the Employer Client (through Employer's Requirements with input from his consultant design team);
· the Contractor Client (through Contractor's Proposals and subsequent development of these, with input from his consultant design team).

2 Coordination and integration
If acting as lead consultant or design team leader appointed by either the Employer Client or the Contractor Client, responsibility for coordinating and integrating the relevant design information may rest with the architect, always depending on the terms of appointment.

3 Employer Client's design in Employer's Requirements
Where an Employer Client includes a scheme devised by his own consultant design team as part of the Employer's Requirements, some Stage E detail work

Fig E.02   **Design information flow: design and build procurement**

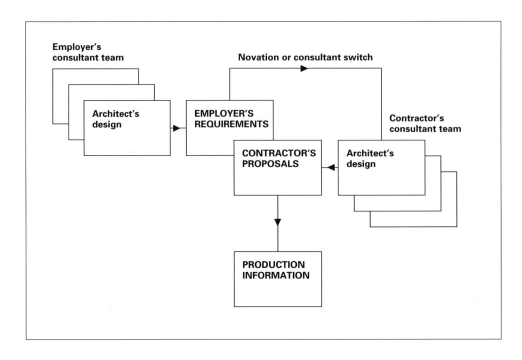

might be relevant. The extent of the commitment should be agreed with the client before work is undertaken. In the event that novation or a 'consultant switch' is envisaged, particular care might be needed to establish design viability. The point of changeover for design liability from one client to the other must be carefully defined.

4 Contractor Client's design in Contractor's Proposals

Where a Contractor Client is expected to offer a scheme design as part of the Contractor's Proposals, this may involve only a fairly limited design exercise, or require a more developed design approach, particularly in the case of two stage tendering. Either way, some exploratory detail design work is necessary to establish the viability of the proposal. The extent of the commitment should be agreed with the client before work is started.

Contractor's Proposals sometimes entail the preparation of a considerable number of architectural drawings – general arrangement, plans, sections and elevations, sectional and elevational details and landscape proposals. There may also be full structural details and a substantial number of services drawings. Obviously effective coordination and integration of the information is very important.

5 Detail design work

Stage E, insofar as it might be relevant for a Contractor Client, could continue intermittently throughout the early stages of construction. It might be difficult to distinguish at times from production information work. Detail design might be subject to fairly liberal interpretation, with last minute amendments, revisions or substitutions by the Contractor Client. He might also have a particular preference for detail design solutions which are familiar, will wish to use materials or components which are available to suit the programme, and wish to keep in line with the estimator's calculations.

Stage E, insofar as it might be relevant for an Employer Client, will probably apply mainly to the development of the Employer's Requirements. Once the contract has been let, any changes in these are likely to be costly and weighted heavily in the contractor's favour.

6 Avoidance of conflict

Once the contract is under way, should any conflict between the Employer's Requirements and the Contractor's Proposals emerge, then depending on the wording of the contract, the latter is likely to take precedence. Careful scrutiny at Stage E is therefore advisable, whether the architect is acting for the Employer Client or the Contractor Client.

Design information flow

Management procurement

Management procurement is likely to be particularly suitable where the project is fairly large or complex, where there is need for early completion, and where the requirements of the client might change or perhaps only be formalised in detail during work on site. Design is still in the hands of the professional team. The Management Contractor is appointed early enough to advise the team on buildability, but carries no responsibility for the design. As lead consultant or design team leader, responsibility for coordinating and integrating information into the overall design rests with the architect, although considerable design input will normally come from the specialist Works Contractors.

1 Origination

Design information can originate from:
- the architect
- professional team members
- specialist Works Contractors.

2 Detail design work

Two general lines of the design will be shown in the Project Drawings and Project Specification produced by the professional team. Some Stage E detail design is an essential precursor to information issued when inviting tenders for works packages.

Further detail design work will arise when the Works Contractors are appointed. Each discrete work package must be placed in the context of the overall design. The information flow can produce management problems if not effectively controlled. Risk of frustrated design work and perhaps abortive fabrication can occur unless agreed procedures are adopted by the Management Contractor and the professional team.

3 Coordination and integration

The Management Contractor can expect to be closely involved in the appointment of Works Contractors. This might be on the basis of developed detail drawings, specifications and perhaps bills of quantities. Drawings prepared by the Works Contractors will be mainly installation or shop drawings, and should be passed to the architect by the Management Contractor for inspection with regard to their integration and incorporation into the overall design.

Fig E.03   **Design information flow: management procurement**

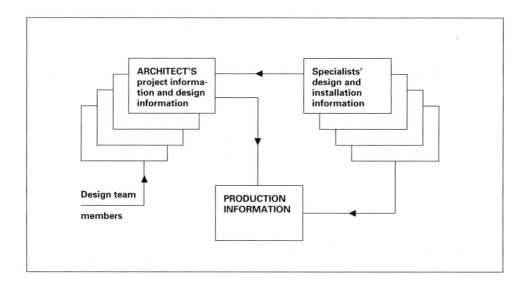

Commencing at Stage E in particular, collaboration between the architect, other members of the design team, and specialists is likely to lead to a regular exchange of drawings. The project quality plan should include procedures for the recording and issue of all drawings, receipt of incoming drawings, and a controlled way of dealing with changes to design decisions already agreed. Fig E.04 is a checklist of the parts of a building for which drawn information might be required.

Register of Drawings

Most practices will already have a standard Register of Drawings, which might record amongst other things:
- job number and title
- drawing number, title, date, revisions (A, B etc)
- scale of drawing, size of drawing (A3, A4 etc)
- number of copies sent, distribution, and date sent.

Where recipients are to be charged for copies, the Register might also allow entries indicating the charge made and by whom payable. In larger practices, or in the case of substantial projects, it might be more practical to open separate Drawings Registers and Print Registers (see Fig E.05).

Schedule of Drawings

Drawing schedules (see Fig E.06) might also serve as convenient and necessary records for several purposes:
- for listing at the start of Stage E what drawings or drawn schedules need to be prepared;
- for listing at the start of Stage F–G what production information needs to be prepared;
- for listing drawings or drawn schedules issued for tender purposes;
- for listing necessary information still to be prepared by the architect and/or the contractor during progress of the works;
- for listing drawings or drawn schedules supplied to the client on completion – either for record purposes or for incorporation in the Health and Safety File.

Drawings Received

A practice should also have its standard record of drawings received. All incoming drawn or scheduled information should be entered, and the sheets might record amongst other things:
- job number and title
- drawing number, title, date, revision
- name of originator
- date received
- whether response required and if so by when
- response made and date achieved.

Drawings Issued

Drawings should never normally be issued simply under cover of a compliments slip. It is better practice to use a Drawing Issue Sheet (see Fig E.07) which indicates the purpose of the action and allows a proper record to be kept.

Design Change Notice

Drawings or other documents indicating proposed design changes should be circulated under cover of a Change Notice (see Fig E.08) which invites comments from recipients. These photocopied (if not sent in duplicate) forms should then be filed and the action taken recorded. Following the adoption of design changes, amendments might be needed to entries in the Register of Drawings.

Fig E.04   **Checklist of necessary drawn information**

Summary		Site layouts General arrangement drawings	
Substructure		Excavation Floor beds	Foundations Pile foundations
Structure	**Primary**	External walls Internal walls Floors and galleries	Stairs and ramps Roofs Frames
	Secondary	External wall openings Internal wall openings Floor openings	Balustrades Suspended ceilings Roof openings
	Finishes	External wall finishes Internal wall finishes Floor finishes	Stair finishes Ceiling finishes Roof finishes
Services	**Piped and ducted**	Refuse disposal Drainage Hot and cold water Gases	Refrigeration Space heating Ventilation and air conditioning
	Electrical	Power Lighting Communications	Transport Security
Fittings	**Fixtures**	Circulation General room Culinary	Sanitary Cleaning Storage
	Loose equipment	Circulation General room Culinary	Sanitary Cleaning Storage
External		Substructure Structure Finishes	Services Fittings

Fig E.05   Specimen registers of drawings and prints

Job no: Job title:

Register of prints

Drawing no.	Drawing title	Issued to	No. copies	Date	Change

Job no: Job title:

Register of drawings

Drawing no.	Drawing title	Scale	Date	Notes

Fig E.06   Specimen schedule of drawings required

Job no: Job title:

Schedule of drawings required
(prepared before drafting starts)

Drawing no.	Drawing title	Sheet size	Scale	Notes
L00	Site location plan	A3	1:1250	
01	Site plan	A1	1:200	
02	Site plan - contractor's fencing	A1	1:200	

Distribution _____ _____ (date)

Fig E.07   **Specimen architect's drawing issue sheet**

Job no: Job title:

Architect's drawing issue sheet

Please find enclosed the drawings listed below.
Any errors or omissions should be notified immediately.

Distribution   No. copies

Purpose of issue   For information ☐   For comment ☐

                   For approval ☐   For cost check ☐

Drawing no.	Revision	Drawing title

Signed _____   _____ (date)

Fig E.08   **Specimen design change notice and record**

Job no: Job title:

Design change notice and record

TO:

Enclosures: Please find enclosed the documents listed below.
Please enter comments, photocopy, and return original notice by

_____ (date)

Issued by _____   _____ (date)

COMMENTS:

Signed _____   _____ (date)

Implementation record   Change adopted   YES/NO   Included in contract   YES/NO

Covered by Architect's Instruction   No.____ issued _____ (date)

Quantity surveyor

The QS should be in close collaboration with the architect during this time of detail design. Choices of materials, and specification notes concerning standards and workmanship need to be watched carefully and checked against the cost plan.

Structural engineer

The engineer should cooperate closely with the architect to ensure a satisfactory integration of structural considerations into the overall design. The engineer should have regard to the location and requirements of all service installations, the building envelope, and the construction process.

Where necessary, the engineer should develop drawings and specifications for tendering documentation for nominated subcontract work or enabling contract works.

Building services engineer

The services engineers should assist the architect in finalising design integration. Their proposals should develop information drawings and specification notes sufficient to allow tendering documentation for nominated subcontract work or nominated supply items.

They should also prepare builders' work requirements in detail for incorporation in the architect's and structural engineer's drawings. All information should be passed to the QS through the architect for checking against the cost plan.

Health and safety

All design team members should cooperate with the Planning Supervisor in providing material to the agreed format for inclusion in the Health and Safety File and to allow completion of the pre-tender Health and Safety Plan.

Production Information and Bills of Quantities

F–G/1   **Activities**

F–G/2   **Actions**

F–G/3   **Stage summary**

F–G/4   **Watchpoints**

F–G/5   **Action checks**

Supplement

F–G/S1   Production information

F–G/S2   Production information: Specification and Schedules of work

F–G/S3   Production information: Bills of quantities

F–G/S4   Building control approval checklist

F–G/S5   Design team roles

Description

At Stages F–G under traditional procurement, the detail design information is translated into precise technical instructions sufficient to allow for pricing and for construction of the proposed works. This information will normally be conveyed by means of written descriptions, drawings and schedules.

Responsibility for production information in design and build procurement is more difficult to establish and will depend on the particular circumstances. It would be very unusual for an Employer Client to arrange for production information direct, although he might require the continued use of his design team by the successful contractor through a consultant switch. The Contractor Client will require production information to be prepared. An architect engaged in this context might well find it advisable to establish exactly how much work, how many drawings etc will be required before agreeing a programme or fee. The contractor might wish to impose restrictions in respect of the method of structuring and supply of production information, preferred technical solutions, materials etc.

With management procurement, the amount of production information available at the commencement of the project will be limited to the extent that much detail information will be supplied by the works contractors by way of shop or installation drawings. Nevertheless the general production information will originate from the professional team, and the process of coordinating and integrating information will continue throughout the construction of the project.

Terminology

* The RIBA Plan of Work refers separately to Stage F Production Information and Stage G Bills of Quantities.

* RIBA standard appointing documents generally refer to Stages F–G Production Information and Bills of Quantities.

* In Design and Build with an Employer Client, Stages F–G might be within the stages termed 'Employer's Requirements'. (These do not normally extend to include production information or bills of quantities, but information relating to such matters might be included.) With a Contractor Client, Stages F–G is still 'Production Information'. (This might be the result of a novation or consultant switch agreement.)

* With Community Architecture projects, the scope of Stages F–G might be extended to include additional User Client requirements concerning organisation and information for self-build groups, semi-skilled labour etc.

General procedures

If coming new to the project at this Stage in the Plan of Work, carry out the relevant Pre-Agreement checks and note any General Procedures listed under earlier Stages which might apply.

If taking over a project on which others were engaged for earlier Plan of Work Stages, allow for familiarisation and checking of all usable material when agreeing fees and timetable with the client.

· Establish the scope and content of Stages F–G. Put it into context, particularly if it follows Stages undertaken by others, or material produced now is likely to be acted upon by others taking over subsequent Stages.

· Agree with the client the extent of professional services for Stages F–G if not yet settled, and confirm in writing.

· Agree with the client the methods and levels of charging for Stages F–G if not yet settled, and confirm in writing.

· Assess the office resources needed for Stages F–G and ensure that they are adequate and available.

· Review the project quality plan, update and develop it as necessary.

· Check progress against the timetable for services regularly.

· Check expenditure against the office job cost allocation for Stages F–G.

· Report regularly to the client on fees and expenses incurred, and submit accounts at agreed intervals.

· Check that the client settles all accounts promptly.

· Check whether the client has any further comments on the detail design as developed at the end of Stage E. It is not always easy or practical to distinguish detail design from production information, but there should be no significant design changes during Stages F–G without client approval.

Design and build

· Check whether the client has confirmed in writing acceptance of proposals and information supplied so far in Stages D–G which are to form part of the Employer's Requirements. *(Employer Client)*

· Review any client's comments on the detail design or development, and note any adjustments which may be unavoidable due to modifications introduced lately by component manufacturers or specialist subcontractors. Detail design amendments might also be necessary because, for example, of substitutes forced by long delivery times. Check what action is to be taken as a result. *(Contractor Client)*

Preliminary issues   **Concerning the client**

· Discuss with the client any outstanding matters of detail design which need to be resolved before preparing production information.

· Check whether any necessary detail information to be supplied by the client is still outstanding.

· Discuss with the client the appointment of subcontractors and specialists at this stage and whether it might be advantageous to place advance orders for materials, design or fabrication. Nomination or naming of subcontractors or suppliers should only be made with the written consent of the client.

· Advise the client on the use of preliminary contracts for enabling works, demolition etc if appropriate.

· Discuss with the client any proposal for work not forming part of the contract to be carried out by other persons (eg the client's own work force) whilst the contractor is in possession. Take account of any such confirmed instructions when preparing production information and programming.

· Advise the client on the need for a clerk of works if appropriate, and explain the role of such a person and appointing procedures.

· Discuss with the client whether interviews with potential contractors should take place at this stage. Under certain circumstances their views on operational methods and health and safety during construction could be valuable. Procurement could also affect how production information is structured or packaged.

· Discuss with the client any intention to impose restrictions on the contractor's working methods (eg sequence, access, limitation on hours, noise etc). This could have an effect on production information and would be essential information for tenderers.

· Discuss with the client essential information for completing contract documents (eg Appendix) and which will need reference in Preliminaries or Preambles of Bills of Quantities/Specification/Schedules of Work.

Concerning other bodies

· Discuss with the Planning Supervisor any outstanding matters of 'designers' contributions to pre-tender Health and Safety Plan including where appropriate site traffic movements and layout for site operations.

· Continue discussions with highways authority on matters such as access to site, waiting or off-loading restrictions, siting and design of temporary fencing, hoardings etc.

· Discuss if appropriate with relevant body (eg English Heritage) protective measures for existing works during site operations.

Preliminary issues
continued

Team working

- Continue to appraise input from specialist firms, including potential subcontractors and suppliers.

- Confirm with design team members arrangements for inviting specialist tenders.

- Obtain from consultants and specialists details of builder's work for installations.

- Draft preliminaries, preambles, specifications for materials and workmanship.

- Consider requirements for commissioning of engineering services by subcontractors, main contractor, and provisions for testing, for inclusion in tender documents.

- Integrate and coordinate input from design team members and specialists, and continue to cooperate with the Planning Supervisor.

- Consolidate final detailed information for production drawings, subcontract specifications and preliminaries to Bills of Quantities/Specification/ Schedules of Work.

- Confirm Stage timetable for services.

- Confirm programme and pattern for design team meetings.

Costs

- Review cost plan and monitor cost implications of decisions during the preparation of production information.

- Review quotations received from specialist firms. Check against provisional sums or budget figures.

Design and build

- Provide revised information if relevant for corrected cost estimates.
  (Employer Client)

- Provide revised information if relevant to contractor's estimators.
  (Contractor Client)

- Continue resource control procedures for office, and monitor expenditure against allocation of fee for Stage.

- Report to the client on cost matters at agreed intervals.

Inspections/tests

- Review quality management of potential suppliers and subcontractors and their general compliance in health and safety matters. Pass relevant information to the Planning Supervisor.

- Decide on the provisions for testing to be included in the Bills of Quantities/Specification/Schedules of Work. Decide on an appropriate provisional sum for inclusion.

- Decide on the provisions for contractor's testing and commissioning of building services before completion, to be included in the Bills of Quantities/Specification/Schedules of Work.

- Determine the provisions for the client's witness testing if required, and whether this is to be part of the contract period. Establish the contractor's obligations for attendance and rectification if necessary.

- Decide on the method statement required from the appointed contractor on quality management testing, verification, audit and records.

Contract

- Confirm with the client the form of contract to be used and Amendments to be incorporated.

- Discuss with the client the need to use Supplements to cover, for example, Sectional Completion, Contractor's Design, Fluctuations etc, and advise.

- Discuss with the client the appropriate choice for optional provisions in the contract. Advise on the particulars which need to be entered in the appendix to the contract, and referred to in the tender documents.

- Check in particular that the client is aware of the requirements of insurance provisions in the contract, and that he appreciates the advisability of seeking specialist advice from his insurers or brokers.

- Discuss with the client the inclusion of any special clauses or amendments to the contract. Advise on the need to take legal advice before amending standard forms of contract.

- Advise the client on the desirability of advance orders for design, materials, and fabrication by specialist subcontractors and suppliers. If authorised, take the necessary action.

- Advise the client on the desirability of preliminary contracts for enabling works, and if authorised take the necessary action.

- Advise the client on the appointment of a clerk of works, and if authorised take the necessary action.

- Discuss with the client any intentions to employ persons direct to carry out work not forming part of the contract during the contractor's occupation, and advise.

Preliminary issues
continued

- Discuss with the client the need to nominate or name specialist subcontractors and suppliers, and advise. If agreed, take appropriate action with regard to inviting tenders.

- Review, with other design team members, tenders received from specialist subcontractors and suppliers. Include in tender documents as appropriate. Cooperate with the Planning Supervisor.

- Discuss tender list for main contract tenders, and when agreed take appropriate action. Cooperate with the Planning Supervisor.

- Draft specification requirements concerning workmanship and materials for inclusion in Bills of Quantities/Specification/Schedules of Work.

- Certify to the Planning Supervisor or the client as appropriate, readiness to proceed to tender.

Design and build

- Advise on completion and content of tender documents and the final form and content of the Employer's Requirements. *(Employer Client)*

- Inspect drawings and information received from specialist subcontractors and suppliers for checking against Contractor's Proposals, and advise the client. *(Contractor Client)*

Stage input

Information necessary during Stages F–G might include the following as relevant:

- Detail design information prepared during Stage E.

- Conditions imposed or amendments recommended by local Building Control and Fire authorities, particularly relating to construction details and fire prevention including finishes.

- Further contributions, information and recommendations from consultants and specialists. In particular, documents submitted by approved subcontractors and suppliers.

- Technical information from manufacturers and recommendations or test results relevant to the particular use intended, context and location.

- Relevant legislation.

Stage output

Tangible results/material produced before the conclusion of Stages F–G might include the following as relevant:

- Production information coordinated documents – probably including location, component and assembly drawings, drawn schedules, Bills of Quantities/Specification/Schedules of Work.

- Information for use in preparing Bills of Quantities/Specification/Schedules of Work – both written and drawn.

- Information prepared specially for use in self-build or semi-skilled operations.

- Information for issue to specialist subcontractors and suppliers in connection with tender invitations.

- Information for preparation of Full Plans submission for approval under Building Regulations.

- Information for inclusion in Health and Safety File – to be passed to the Planning Supervisor.

- Information for inclusion in pre-tender Health and Safety Plan – to be passed to the Planning Supervisor.

- Non-production information for use in dealings with third parties, landlords, tenants, funders etc (eg in connection with leases, boundaries, party walls etc).

Design and build

- Detail design information for incorporation into Employer's Requirements (part of Stages D–G). *(Employer Client)*

- General arrangement drawings, interface details, performance specification and other technical information (part of Stages F–G). *(Contractor Client)*

* From now on any changes made to the brief, even apparently minor ones, might cause delay and abortive work. The client should be warned of this.

* Approval under building regulations should be sought at the earliest opportunity and clearance secured in respect of compliance with Fire Codes etc.

* Encourage the QS to adopt a formal approach to 'question-and-answer' procedures as soon as possible. Ask him to state his priorities for receiving information for billing purposes.

* Adopt the Common Arrangement for production information wherever practicable and see that other design team members do the same.

* Check information against current legislation, codes and standards before completing drawings.

* Obtain necessary information in good time from firms to be named or nominated, and place reliance on it only after having secured a design warranty in favour of the client.

* Monitor all information originating from consultants and specialists. As lead consultant you are responsible for its coordination and integration into the general scheme.

* Establish a cut-off point for information to be passed to the QS. This will become information for tenderers. Any subsequent changes are then to be treated formally as contract variations at the appropriate time.

* Use standard specification clauses which are clear and precise. It should be normal practice to use the appropriate version of NBS.

* Use a specification in addition to bills of quantities by incorporating it so that it forms part of the contract documentation.

* Check on availability and delivery before including particular materials or sources named in production information.

* If advance orders seem desirable, make a recommendation to the client and obtain authorisation before taking action.

* Check with the client contract particulars to be included in information for tenderers, eg dates, insurances, liquidated damages, option clauses etc.

* Take care when including provisional sums that the figure is adequate, and that wherever possible it is for defined work.

* Remember that the pre-tender Health and Safety Plan, as prepared by the Planning Supervisor, will need to be issued at tender stage.

		Tick if relevant	Initial if completed
01	Establish scope, content and context for Stage activities		
02	Check client's written instruction to proceed		
03	If coming new to project, refer to previous Stage checks		
04	Check appointing documents wrt services and fees		
05	Check client has settled all accounts submitted to date		
06	Review and develop project quality plan as necessary		
07	Check office resources wrt services, timetable, fee		
08	Review with design team implications of any design changes		
09	Review with consultants' etc services, timetable etc		
10	Check all necessary/latest Codes, Standards etc are available		
11	Check all necessary statutory and other consents obtained		
12	Obtain from S/Cs, suppliers any outstanding project info.		
13	Check user client needs wrt info., self-build, unskilled labour		
14	Check with client any phasing, restrictions and implications		
15	Check with client any special or optional contract provisions		
16	Check with client and advisers on insurance for works etc		
17	Check with client details for contract Appendix entries		
18	Check with client names of specialists for Bills/Spec/Schedules		
19	Check information wrt provisional sums for Bills etc		
20	Complete info. wrt prescriptive/performance items in Bills etc		
21	Check draft Bills/Specification/Schedules of Work		
22	Check designers' cooperation with P/S wrt H & S Plan and File		
23	Collate information from consultants and specialists		
24	Review cost plan and implications of production info. decisions		
25	Monitor office expenditure against fee income		
26	Confirm with client and P/S main contract tender list etc		
27	Check with client arrangements for appointing clerk of works		
28	Take action on advance ordering as authorised		
29	Certify readiness to proceed to tender to client and P/S		
30			

Supplement

F–G

F–G/S1   **Production information**

F–G/S2   **Production information: Specification and Schedules of work**

F–G/S3   **Production information: Bills of quantities**

F–G/S4   **Building control approval checklist**

F–G/S5   **Design team roles**

Standard procedures and methods of work

Standard procedures should be agreed with the design team at the earliest opportunity, in relation to:
- Drawings classification, scales, sizes, annotations etc.
- Use of base and copy negatives, overlay draughting, photo drawings etc.
- Use of computer-aided draughting and layering of information.
- Structuring of information, eg location, assembly, component drawings, drawn schedules.
- Incorporation of feedback from previous experience.
- Incorporation of information from client, specialist subcontractors and suppliers, other sources.
- Timetable for production information.

Architects producing drawings and drawn schedules should:
- Draft a schedule of drawings and other information needed.
- Work out a realistic timetable, after assessing the amount of work involved and resources available.
- Confirm a system for recording and distributing information and revisions.
- Arrange for printed sheets, title panels etc as appropriate.
- Compile specification notes as relevant during the production of drawn information.

Drawings at Stages F–G

Drawings at this Stage are produced for three main reasons:
- because they must accompany bills of quantities for tendering purposes as stipulated by SMM7;
- because they will later become contract documents;
- because they may need to be developed or issued as other 'necessary information' to the main contractor when work on site commences.

The number of drawings required is likely to be influenced by the size of the project, the procurement method to be adopted (ie who actually produces the drawings), and the relative significance of drawn information in relation to other contract documents.

Structuring architects' drawings

Architects' drawings are best structured as follows.

Location drawings (for example, block plan, site plan, general arrangement plans, sections, elevations).

Where the project is so large that at a suitable scale these will not fit easily on to single sheets, it might be necessary to split the project into suitable blocks or zones. They should enable users to gain an overall picture of the building, give setting-out dimensions, locate and identify the parts of the building, and refer out to more specific information.

Assembly drawings
These will be divided into groups representing parts of the building, eg walls, stairs, roofs, openings, ceilings, fittings, external works. They should show the construction of the building, particularly at selected junctions, and refer out to more specific information as necessary.

Component drawings (eg purpose-made windows, doors).
These should be referred to from the location drawings. They should show the shape, dimensions and assembly of various parts, and identify components which are not described adequately elsewhere.

Drawings from the structural engineer and the building services engineers should be structured in a compatible manner despite the fact that information in their cases is likely to come from a number of sources, including specialist subcontractors and suppliers.

Purpose of drawings

Whatever drawings are produced it is important to be clear about their intended purpose and the needs of the user of the drawing. Any drawing should provide such information as shape or profile, dimensions (notional or finished), position, composition and relation to other parts including tolerances, fixing methods etc. On a small project where only a small number of drawings is necessary, these might embrace the needs of all trades and suppliers and be annotated to the extent that no other supporting document is required.

Conversely, larger projects will require a considerable number of drawings and schedules, each devised with a particular trade or element in mind, and cross-referencing to other drawings will need to be carried out with great care.

A checklist of the parts of a building which may need to be covered in a production information drawing and schedule programme is given as Fig E.04.

Drawn schedules

In addition to the drawings, some information is more clearly and conveniently conveyed in drawn schedule form. Schedules commonly include:
- Ironmongery (with location and fixings)
- Doors
- Windows (to include glazing)
- Finishes (floor, walls, ceilings)
- Precast lintols and cills
- Inspection chambers and manhole covers
- Colours.

Any elements or components which are repetitive or can be grouped may be suitable for scheduling. The exercise is a good coverage check for compilers, but information should not be repeated on the drawings as this might lead to confusion and inconsistencies.

**Coordinated
Project Information**

The Latham Report, *Constructing the Team*, gives strong support for the adoption of Coordinated Project Information (CPI) for all projects regardless of procurement method. The CPI publication, *Production Drawings*, provides a code of procedure which should be followed wherever possible. The code is for use by all members of the design team who have the task of preparing and issuing production drawings. It is complementary to BS 1192:1984, *Construction Drawing Practice*.

Production information: Specification and Schedules of work

Specification

The architect as designer should be responsible for the method of specification selected, and the content. Specification notes will normally be compiled during the design process. The specification is a key document and will provide information to:
- the contractor's estimator when preparing a tender;
- the QS when preparing bills of quantities;
- the clerk of works or contractor during construction work.

Members of the design team might prepare the specification for those parts of the work which require specialist knowledge, but the architect as design team leader should remain responsible for overall content and coordination.

A specification is a written document which may describe the materials or products to be used, standards of workmanship required, performance requirements, and the conditions under which the work will be carried out.

Specification can be prescriptive, in that there is precise reference to standards set out elsewhere in a published document (eg natural slates to BS 680: Part 2), or because a full description of workmanship, appearances etc to be achieved is given.

Specification can also be by stated performance requirements either for the building components or engineering services. A specification can be a contract document where there is no bill of quantities. As such it might be fairly general in coverage, with the tenderer only expected to produce a contract sum, albeit supported by a schedule of rates. A specification can be itemised to the extent that it becomes a priceable document, and would then form a 'priced document' for the purpose of valuing variations during the contract.

A specification will usually be needed even when there is a separate bill of quantities. CPI advocates giving it contract document status by making it part of the bill. This can be done by calling the specification 'Bill Number 2'. Alternatively it can be done by introducing the relevant parts of the specification as preambles to the various measured work sections of the bill of quantities.

Schedules of work

Schedules of work comprise lists of the various items of work to be carried out, usually on a room by room basis. It is customary to introduce a number or area alongside the items to encourage systematic pricing by tenderers. Items in respect of each room are usually listed under headings such as doors, ceilings, wall finishes, floor finishes, fittings. Schedules of work should not contain quantities, for they are not exact documents by nature. A contractor when pricing should be expected to include for everything necessary to complete the works.

Schedules of work might be a contract document where there is no bill of quantities. They are sometimes regarded as an alternative to a specification, particularly when used for housing refurbishment or alteration work. However, there is often a strong case for having a specification in addition to the schedule.

Actions for architects

Architects responsible for the preparation of specifications should:
- Agree with the design team a strategy including a programme for the production of appropriate documents (eg specification/schedules/bill of quantities).
- Assemble specification notes during detail design Stage E.
- Prepare a checklist to show which headings or subheadings might be relevant for the particular project.
- Select from the library of standard specification clauses (preferably NBS).
- Identify sections or items which are not covered adequately and which will require special draughting.
- Allocate responsibilities for writing particular parts of the specification.
- Establish which parts will be by prescription and which by performance requirements.
- If specifying by reference, obtain the documents and carefully read the relevant parts.
- Review selection of materials, descriptions of workmanship etc and check with cost plan.
- Mark up library of clauses and produce a draft copy of the specification.
- Decide on presentation of the specification.
- Check final copy for errors, omissions and possible inconsistencies either within parts of the document or between the specification and other production information.
- Establish the number of copies required and distribute as appropriate.

CPI procedures

The introduction of Coordinated Project Information (CPI) procedures has created an efficient way of achieving integrated architectural and engineering drawings, specifications and bills of quantities. The common arrangement of work sections for building works (CAWS) has been adopted throughout the documents. The National Building Specification (NBS), National Engineering Specification (NES) and the Standard Method of Measurement (SMM7) all use this arrangement. The architect and the QS will find it easier to prepare and interpret a specification where it shares a common arrangement with the method of measurement used in preparing the bills.

Some architects' practices might use a system of specification clauses developed for use with particular types of work (eg housing refurbishment). Care must be taken to keep such clauses relevant and up to date, and it is generally safer and more convenient to adopt a well-developed system such as NBS. This allows for consistent description of materials and workmanship with full reference to British Standards and other codes and standards. NBS also enables performance specifications to be developed.

NBS is available in hard copy or software in Full, Abridged or Minor Works versions. The CPI publication, *Project Specification*, provides a code of procedure which should be followed wherever possible.

Pricing a Bill of Quantities is the traditional method of obtaining comparable tenders for projects where the design has been fully detailed beforehand. Where an accurate or full Bill of Quantities becomes part of the contract documentation, it usually means that quality and quantity included for in the price will be as that stated in the Contract Bills. It is therefore important to ensure that the Bill is full, accurately reflects the intentions of the architect, and does not conflict with information shown on the drawings.

Notional bills or approximate quantities

Where is it not possible to present the QS with a completely detailed design and specification, it may be possible to invite tenders on the basis of notional bills or approximate quantities. These should be reasonably accurate as to description and items, with only the amounts left subject to measurement after completion.

Work which cannot be quantified with certainty, even in an accurate Bill of Quantities, may be covered by the introduction of provisional sums (for either defined or undefined work), prime cost sums (where an accurate figure can be placed on a subcontract or supply item), or an approximate quantity (where the item is certain but the quantity is not). The once frequent inclusion of a contingency sum is nothing more than a provisional figure for undefined work of an unforeseeable nature. All such items require later instructions from the architect before the contractor can act on them.

Standard Method of Measurement

A uniform basis of measuring work for inclusion in a Bill of Quantities may be found in the Standard Method of Measurement of Building Works, currently in a seventh edition (SMM7). Although it is usually the prerogative of the QS to decide which method of measurement to adopt and how the bill will be structured, for building work this is most likely to be using the Common Arrangement, and in accordance with SMM7. The contents of a bill prepared in this way are likely to include:

Preliminaries/General conditions
· Items which are not specific to work sections but which have an identifiable cost (eg site facilities, insurances).
· Items for fixed and time related costs (eg plant, temporary works).

Work sections
(also incorporating cross-references to drawings and specification)
C   Demolition/alteration/renovation
D   Groundwork
E   In situ concrete/large precast concrete
F   Masonry – brick, block, stonework etc
G   Structural/carcassing – metal and timber
H   Cladding/covering – patent glazing, plastics etc
J   Waterproofing
K   Linings/dry partitions
L   Windows/doors/stairs
M   Surface finishes – screeds, tiling, decorating etc
P   Building fabric sundries – trims, ironmongery etc
Q   Paving/planting/fencing/outdoor furniture
R   Disposal systems – pipework gutters, drainage
Y   Mechanical and electrical services.

To assist the QS during preparation of the Bill, the architect might be expected to supply the following.

· Specification or specification notes for incorporation as preambles to work sections.
· Information for inclusion in Preliminaries such as
  – form of contract, supplements, option clauses, amended clauses etc
  – content and use of contract documentation
  – method statements required
  – pre-tender Health and Safety Plan
  – work to be done by employer direct
  – requirements concerning sequence, time limitations etc
  – provisional sums to be included
  – provision for named/nominated subcontractors/suppliers.
· Diagrams for inclusion in the Bill (eg extent of retaining structures, cornice profiles, multi-coloured paintwork etc). SMM7 Rule 5.3 refers to the use of dimensioned diagrams in place of a dimensioned description.
· Drawn information to accompany the Bill:
  – location drawings (ie block plan, site plan, floor plans, sections and elevations);
  – component drawings (ie showing information necessary for manufacture and assembly);
  – drawn schedules;
· Dimensions, which will normally appear on the drawings listed above. In particular the QS will require overall dimensions, and internal dimensions of all rooms and spaces.

SMM7 Rules 5.1, 5.2 and 5.4 refer to drawn information. These might be expected to apply to most of the Work Sections listed above. In many cases it will simply show the scope and location of the work. In other cases (eg E, H etc) it will require the supply of detail drawings.

The QS will almost certainly expect a rapid response to the Query Sheets directed at the architect during Bill preparations. It will also assist the QS if information is despatched to suit the taking-off process, that is, to ensure that the right information is received in the right sequence.

The CPI publication, *SMM7*, contains a full set of the General Rules. There is also the *SMM7 Measurement Code* published by CPI which includes a commentary on particular rules and contains illustrative material likely to be of assistance to the architect.

Building control approval checklist

Preparing an application for Building Regulations approval is normally one of the services provided by the architect. In many cases, although informal consultations may well have taken place earlier, the drawings and calculations necessary to support a formal submission will not be sufficiently developed until well into Production Information.

For England and Wales, the principal legislation is The Building Act 1984, which empowered the making of Building Regulations (currently 1991). Health and Safety legislation is quite separate, as is Fire Precautions legislation. These latter areas of law, although administered by different authorities, closely affect building and should be regarded as complementary.

Approval procedures

Building Regulations approval may be sought by application to the local authority using either the Full Plans or the Building Notice procedure. Using the former means that you can seek a Determination if you consider that your work complies with the Regulations, or a Dispensation if you consider that the strict legal requirements are too onerous in a particular set of circumstances. Using the Building Notice procedure means that you do not have to submit full plans but you must be reasonably confident that the work complies, because there is no opportunity to seek a Determination.

If you elect to use an Approved Inspector and not make application to the local authority, then you follow the Initial Notice procedure. This takes the place of both the local authorities procedures described above.

The Building Regulations 1991

The Regulations include for the following.

Regulation 4 states the requirements relating to building work. It refers to Schedule 1 which sets out the Functional Requirements, and it is the 'practical guidance' on meeting these requirements which is found in the Approved Documents (S6 Building Act 1984). Regulation 4 refers to building work, and Regulation 6 extends the application to material change of use.

Regulation 9 states that the Building Regulations will not apply to all building work, and the exemptions (mostly uninhabitable, small, temporary or ancillary buildings) are set out in Schedule 2.

Regulation 8 makes it clear that there is a legal obligation to go beyond that which is necessary to secure reasonable standards of health and safety for persons in or about buildings. It may include the welfare and convenience of persons. It may also include for conservation of fuel and power, prevention of waste etc.

Regulation 7 supplements the requirements of Schedule 1 and is concerned with materials and workmanship. Architects should carefully consider what to specify and contractors should ensure that specified standards are achieved by effective quality control. The Approved Document on materials and workmanship is very general. Guidance is given on fitness and adequacy by reference to past experience, Agrément Certificates, British Standards, EC Construction Products Directives and testing. The emphasis seems to be on selecting materials and methods that are known and proven. In the event of a failure, it would be for the architect to demonstrate that the requirements of Regulation 7 have been met.

Regulation 10 establishes that applications for relaxation or a dispensation may be made to the local authority. An appeal may be made to the Secretary of State.

Regulations 1–15 set out the procedural requirements where application for approval is made to the local authority. If the application is made to an Approved Inspector, then the Building (Approved Inspectors etc) Regulations will apply.

Applications to the local authority may be by Full Plans (Regulation 13) or Building Notice (Regulation 12). The latter is not an option where the proposed work is in shops or offices, or is subject to rules for means of escape in the event of fire.

The technical requirements under the Building Regulations are set out in Schedule 1. They aim to ensure that buildings meet reasonable standards of health and safety, although additionally Part L is concerned with energy conservation and Part M is concerned with access for the disabled. The requirements are stated in broad terms of performance standards, and guidance as to what might satisfy these are given in the Approved Documents.

Submitting an application

When preparing or submitting an application to the local authority, note the following.
- Assuming that the work is not 'exempt' (check against Building Reg 9 and Schedule 2), either deposit Full Plans (Regs 11–14) or give a Building Notice in the case of small works.
- A prescribed fee is payable. This is revised fairly frequently. Check with the local authority.
- The Secretary of State has power (through the local authority) to dispense with or relax a Regulation (see S8 Building Act 1984), and to make Determinations (S16).
- The local authority must pass or reject a Full Plans application within five weeks (unless a longer period not exceeding eight weeks is agreed).
- The local authority must be given two days' notice before commencement of work, one day's notice must be given before certain work is covered up, and notice is required within five days of completion.
- Where work is not commenced within three years of approval, the local authority may hold that the notices or deposited plans are of no effect (S32 Building Act 1984).
- When work is carried out without Building Regulations approval, or in contravention of the Regulations, the local authority is empowered to require its removal or alteration to comply. The local authority may, if necessary, seek a court injunction.

Quantity surveyor

The QS should be supplied with drawings and specifications for all the contract works. Any observed discrepancies or omissions should be raised with the architect, preferably by question-and-answer sheets. The QS will carry out cost checks and keep the architect informed of the results. Contract particulars and other information for the preliminaries should be supplied to the QS. Once the billing and tendering documentation is complete, the QS should provide the design team with an up to date estimate for the project.

Structural engineer

The engineer should prepare production drawings and specifications for the relevant construction and operations on site. Documents might also be needed for preliminary contracts or enabling works which usually have a structural content.

The engineer should provide the QS with drawings and specifications for billing, and with reinforcement lists or schedules as relevant. It might also be necessary to supply copies of surveys, soil reports and geotechnical information to accompany tender enquiries.

Building services engineer

The services engineers should prepare the necessary drawings and specification. Tendering procedures for named or nominated subcontract work should be finalised. Where work is to be subject to performance specification and is intended to be the direct responsibility of the main contractor, albeit via some domestic arrangement, then this must be covered in a full and satisfactory manner.

All necessary information should be passed to the QS for inclusion in the specification and bill of quantities. Where the services engineers are responsible for obtaining tenders from subcontractors and suppliers, evaluation of these should be in collaboration with the architect, QS, and Planning Supervisor.

Health and safety

All design team members should cooperate with the Planning Supervisor in providing material to the agreed format for inclusion in the Health and Safety File and to allow completion of the pre-tender Health and Safety Plan.

Tender Action H

H/1   **Activities**

H/2   **Actions**

H/3   **Stage summary**

H/4   **Watchpoints**

H/5   **Action checks**

Supplement

H/S1   Selective tendering lists

H/S2   Selective tendering: Specialist subcontractors and suppliers

H/S3   Selective tendering: Main contract – Traditional procurement

H/S4   Selective tendering: Main contract – Design and build procurement

H/S5   Selective tendering: Main contract – Management procurement

Description

Tendering is an activity not wholly confined to Stage H. For example, there will often be need to obtain tenders from specialist subcontractors or suppliers at an earlier stage. Sometimes it may be advantageous if the main contractor is appointed earlier to advise pre-construction. Obviously the procurement method adopted, or the size and complexity of the project, can have an effect on tender action and timing. Normally however, Stage H is when the main contract tenders are invited, evaluated, and advice given to the client on appointing the contractor.

Tenders may be obtained by following one of these routes:

- Open tendering – open to all and in theory competitive, but generally regarded as wasteful, often unreliable, and not in the client's long term interests.

- Selective tendering – open to selected invitees only, competitive, and appropriate for all forms of procurement.

- Negotiated tendering – applicable where price is not the main criterion, and not necessarily competitive except perhaps where it forms the second step in a two stage process.

Tendering will mostly be a single stage activity, but where the project is particularly large and complex, or where the procurement method makes it desirable, then two stage tendering can be a more efficient and satisfactory way forward.

Regardless of the route chosen, it is important to ensure that tendering is always on a fair basis. Competition should only be between firms who have the necessary skills, integrity, responsibility and reputation which will enable them to deliver work of the nature and standard required. Competitive tendering should involve only a realistic number of bids, from firms who have been given the same information, and the same realistic period in which to formulate offers.

It is sound practice always to follow the relevant Guidance Notes and Codes of Procedures published by the National Joint Consultative Committee for Building (NJCC), which are agreed within the construction industry, and endorsed without reservation in the Latham Report, *Constructing the Team*. Tendering in the local or public authority sectors may also be subject to standing orders, and the Public Works Contracts Regulations 1991 and any subsequent legislation.

Refer to current issues of the following NJCC publications:

- Code of Procedure for Single Stage Selective Tendering

- Code of Procedure for Two Stage Selective Tendering

- Code of Procedure for Selective Tendering for Design and Build

- Code of Procedure for Selection of a Management Contractor

- Guidance Note 1: Joint Venture Tendering

- Guidance Note 2: Performance Bonds

· Guidance Note 4: Pre-Tender Meetings

· Guidance Note 8: Selection and Appointment of Construction Manager and Trade Contractors.

Terminology

* The RIBA Plan of Work refers to Stage H Tender Action.

* RIBA standard appointing documents generally also refer to Stage H Tender Action.

* In Design and Build with an Employer Client, Stage H is Tender Action, and with a Contractor Client Stage H is also Tender Action but it follows immediately after Stage C Contractor's Proposals. (There is normally no Stage J identified with the Contractor Client version of Design and Build.)

General procedures

If coming new to the project at this Stage in the Plan of Work, carry out the relevant Pre-Agreement checks and note any General Procedures listed under earlier Stages which might apply.

If taking over a project on which others were engaged for earlier Plan of Work Stages, allow for familiarisation and checking of all usable material when agreeing fees and timetable with the client.

- Establish the scope and content of Stage H. Put it into context, particularly if it follows Stages undertaken by others, or material produced is likely to be acted upon by others taking over subsequent Stages.

- Agree with the client the extent of professional services for Stage H if not yet settled, and confirm in writing.

- Agree with the client the methods and levels of charging for Stage H if not yet settled, and confirm in writing.

- Assess the office resources needed for Stage H and ensure that they are adequate and available.

- Review the project quality plan, update and develop it as necessary.

- Check progress against the timetable for services regularly.

- Check expenditure against the office job cost allocation for Stage H.

- Report regularly to the client on fees and expenses incurred, and submit accounts at agreed intervals.

- Check that the client settles all accounts promptly.

- Check whether the client has confirmed in writing acceptance of the recommended method of appointing the main contractor – by negotiation, by competition, or a combination of both.

- Check that the client accepts the time and cost factor where interviews or pre-tender meetings with potential contractors are appropriate.

- Check the extent to which the Planning Supervisor expects to be involved in tendering procedures.

Preliminary issues

Concerning the client

- Check with the client whether tendering for the particular project is likely to be subject to legislative control. This could have an effect on procurement methods and procedures.

- Check whether the client has firm views on the preferred tendering method, and names to be considered for inclusion on a tender list.

- Check whether the client holds a General List of Approved Contractors from which tenderers must be selected.

Preliminary issues
continued

- Discuss with the client whether firms who wish to be considered as tenderers should complete a tendering questionnaire (eg NJCC Standard Form of Tendering Questionnaire).

- Check whether the client will require tenderers to complete a non-collusion or other similar certificate.

- Agree with the client and the Planning Supervisor the tendering period, procedures to be followed in opening tenders and notifying results.

- Check with the client that the site will be available to the contractor on the date stated in the documents, and that there is nothing likely to prevent possession or commencement.

Team working

- Check with design team members their input to main contract tender documents to discover inconsistencies, errors or omissions.

- Check with design team members tenders and accompanying information received from specialist subcontractors and suppliers and if acceptable approve them.

- Confirm Stage timetable for services.

- Confirm programme and pattern for any further meetings of the design team.

Costs

- Check with quantity surveyor for cost appraisal immediately before sending out documents to tenderers. Report to client if appropriate.

- Check with quantity surveyor for arithmetical errors in the most acceptable tender and if any are found, use the appropriate stated procedures. Ask the tenderer which course of action he prefers to follow.

- Report to the client after the QS has examined the tenders and make recommendations about acceptance.

- Discuss with the QS the most appropriate measures for reducing the lowest figure, if this proves necessary.

- Continue resource control procedures for office, and monitor expenditure against allocation of fee for Stage.

Inspections/tests

- Arrange for tenderers to have the opportunity to inspect the site and/or existing buildings during the tender period.

- Arrange for tenderers to have the opportunity to inspect drawings not issued with the tender documents.

· Inspect draft programmes submitted by tenderers, if required.

· Arrange for the Planning Supervisor to inspect material submitted by tenderers relating to health and safety requirements, and to appraise the construction phase Health and Safety Plan submitted by the most acceptable tenderer.

Contract

· Send out preliminary enquiries to firms selected as potential tenderers, as agreed with the client.

· Invite tenders for main contract works from firms who have accepted the invitation to tender.

· Appraise with QS tenders received and prepare a report with recommendations for the client.

· Check willingness and availability of firms included as listed subcontractors, and if necessary decide on additional names.

· Assist as necessary with negotiations following consideration by the client of the most acceptable tender.

· Continue with appraisal of tenders from specialists. Check that offers are still open for acceptance and that particulars on which they tendered are still correct.

· Arrange for interviews, if appropriate, for selection of contractors by negotiation.

· Check that Planning Supervisor has certified that the Health and Safety Plan has been developed sufficiently by the firm to be appointed as Principal Contractor for the construction phase to commence.

Design and build

· Assist client with negotiations following submission of Contractor's Proposals and Contract Sum Analysis as relevant. This might be equally relevant whether acting for an Employer Client or a Contractor Client. *(Employer Client, Contractor Client)*

Stage input

Information necessary during Stage H might include the following as relevant:

- Production information coordinated documents, complete and ready for despatch to invited tenderers.

- Pre-tender Health and Safety Plan.

- Tender list as agreed with client.

- Completed tender documents from nominated or named subcontractors and suppliers with all sections properly completed.

- Relevant published procedure notes and guidance on selected method of tendering (eg NJCC).

- Completed particulars for contract, and for Supplements to form of contract.

- Cost appraisal prepared by QS based on Bills of Quantities/Specification/ Schedules of Work.

Stage output

Tangible results/material produced before the conclusion of Stage H might include the following as relevant:

- Information for inclusion in contract documentation: option clauses, special or amended clauses, appendix entries.

- Approved list of main contract tenderers and prepared tender documents.

- Tenders received from specialists with appropriate forms (eg NAM/T, NSC/T) and 'numbered documents' where appropriate.

- Secondary negatives or disks with information issued for convenience and accuracy to main contract tenderers seeking subcontract tenders.

- Main contract tenders, and report with recommendations.

Design and build

- Report for client on appraisal of Contractor's Proposals and Contract Sum Analysis. *(Employer Client)*

- Report for client on appraisal of tenders submitted by specialist subcontractors and suppliers. *(Contractor Client)*

- Final material for incorporation into Contractor's Proposals and in connection with Contract Sum Analysis. *(Contractor Client)*

---

* Tender lists should only include firms well known to the architect, or firms which have been satisfactorily investigated.

* When inviting tenders for specialist subcontract work which includes a design element, make certain that the client consents in writing, and that his interests are properly protected by warranty.

* Follow meticulously the procedures stated in the contract for the appointment of specialist subcontractors.

* Check that numbered documents sufficiently explain the requirements, that they are accurate, listed and numbered.

* Check that drawings required under SMM7 Measurement Code are ready to accompany Bills to tenderers.

* Follow the relevant NJCC Codes of Procedure for Tendering to ensure fairness and reliable pricing.

* Supply all tenderers with identical information. If queries are raised during the tendering period, deal with them promptly and notify all other tenderers in identical terms.

* Any requirements for a warranty or guarantee bond must be made known to tenderers at the time of invitation.

* Allow adequate time for tendering, and for the assessment of tenders. The most acceptable tender must be thoroughly checked for errors, and this takes time.

* Allow time for checking by the Planning Supervisor.

* Pre-tender meetings and interviews should only be held if considered essential, and always with a strictly limited agenda.

* Do not accept late tenders.

* Refer specialist tenders to Planning Supervisor and relevant consultants for comment. Refer all tenders to the QS for cost checking.

* Be wary of a very low tender. Explain to the client the possible risks in accepting it.

* Deal with tender errors, or the need for a reduction, strictly in accordance with the relevant NJCC Code of Procedure.

* Inform unsuccessful tenderers of the outcome at the earliest opportunity and provide figures when appropriate.

* Only place advance orders with specialist subcontractors or suppliers as provided for in the subcontract documentation, and only if authorised in writing by the client, as advised by the Planning Supervisor.

Action checks

		Tick if relevant	Initial if completed
01	Establish scope, content and context for Stage activities		
02	Check client's written instruction to proceed		
03	If coming new to project, refer to previous Stage checks		
04	Check appointing documents wrt services and fees		
05	Check client has settled all accounts submitted to date		
06	Review and develop project quality plan as necessary		
07	Check office resources wrt services, timetable, fee		
08	Review/update standing lists or register of tenderers		
09	Check tender invitation documents for sending to specialists		
10	Invite or check for validity tenders from specialists		
11	Review specialists' tenders with consultants and P/S		
12	Approve specialist tenders and notify all tenderers of decision		
13	Collate and check information for main contract tenders		
14	Invite tenders for main contract		
15	Review with client tenders from main contractors		
16	Refer acceptable tenderers' documents to QS and P/S		
17	Arrange interviews to select Principal Contractor if relevant		
18	Initiate action for second stage tendering if relevant		
19	Initiate action for reduction of tender figure if relevant		
20	Notify unsuccessful tenderers of result		
21	Release information about tender results when contract signed		
22	Monitor office expenditure against fee income		
23			
24			
25			
26			
27			
28			
29			
30			

Supplement

H

H/S1   **Selective tendering lists**

H/S2   **Selective tendering: Specialist subcontractors and suppliers**

H/S3   **Selective tendering: Main contract – Traditional procurement**

H/S4   **Selective tendering: Main contract – Design and build procurement**

H/S5   **Selective tendering: Main contract – Management procurement**

Selective tendering lists

Contractors and specialist subcontractors invited to tender must have experience properly suited to the project. They should be selected to compete on equal terms.

Selected contractors may be expected to provide information about their firms and their track records. Architects will then wish to take up references and make further enquiries about those who seem suitable for inclusion in shortlists. It is advisable to maintain a file or record of all enquiries to contractors and subcontractors and their responses.

Lists of potential contractors can be as follows:

Shortlist of contractors for small projects

Contractors known by reputation or from previous experience. Compiled after consulting the client, office records and other sources. Discuss with QS and other consultants as appropriate. Enter names agreed by the client.

Select list of contractors for larger projects

Compiled after responses to questionnaire sent to potential tenderers for one particular contract. The questionnaire might be expected to cover:
· name and details of company;
· business status of company, names of directors etc;
· financial status, share capital ctc;
· details of quality system and accreditation;
· details of insurers and liability insurance;
· construction turnover and details of contracts completed recently;
· names of three referees;
· Health and Safety policy and procedures;
· policy on discrimination.

The completed questionnaire should be signed by a director of the company.

The NJCC publishes a Standard Form of Tendering Questionnaire, 'Application for admission to select lists of contractors for one particular contract'.

Approved standing list of contractors

Compiled after responses to questionnaire sent to potential tenderers. Shortlists of tenderers for future particular projects can then be drawn up as and when required.

The questionnaire might be expected to include the information shown above, with additional entries to indicate the type of work the firm has experience of, and whether they would be interested in tendering for non-traditional procurement contracts.

The NJCC publishes a Standard Form of Tendering Questionnaire, 'Application for admission to approved lists of contractors'.

Identify items

During the detail design and production information stages, items where a measure of control over choice needs to be exercised should be identified. These might include for example:

- materials or suppliers named or nominated;
- acceptable subcontractors restricted to listed names;
- subcontractors named or nominated, as provided for by the contract.

Where subcontractors or suppliers have been nominated or named under procedures laid down in the particular contract, there is usually a requirement or opportunity to use a standard design warranty in favour of the Employer. However where subcontractors or suppliers are referred to in items in the Bill or Specification and are intended to be domestic appointments, then the contractor will have no liability for their design input. In such cases the employer's interests might need to be protected by a warranty, should this be available. The client's consent should always be obtained in writing where subcontractors have a design input which might be regarded as subcontracting by the architect.

The purpose of tendering should be identified, eg whether it is to obtain information necessary to complete detail design, to obtain a realistic basis for a provisional sum, or to facilitate advance ordering, where desirable.

List suitable firms

Compile a list after discussion with other members of the design team, and the contractor (if appointed). Refer to office records of previous experience, and check out references if necessary.

Make preliminary enquiries

Consult the QS and other consultants to establish a timetable for inviting tenders so as to provide necessary information for inclusion in bills/specification/schedules.

Check that current information is obtained concerning the financial status of firms, and that they have adequate resources.

Send a preliminary invitation to tender, or to ascertain willingness for inclusion in a list of subcontractors or as a named supplier. If approximate dates and figures can be given at this stage, it should be possible to obtain a reliable response. See specimen letter, Fig H.01.

Invite tenders

Use the correct standard forms appropriate to the form of contract (eg NSC/T or NAM/T etc) and check that all relevant information is entered before sending.

Check the Information to be issued with the tender form, in particular the numbered documents (eg drawings, schedules, Bills or specification) relevant to the subcontract works. They should adequately define the work to be tendered for. A covering letter may or may not be considered necessary.

If the subcontract work is such that no particular form or set of procedures is required under the terms of the main contract, then send tender information under a suitable enclosing letter. See specimen letter, Fig H.02.

Deal with tenders

Tenders should be opened as soon as possible after the date for receipt. Check that everything specified has been included. Note any omissions or added conditions and pass to relevant consultants for comment, and to QS for cost checking.

Approve the selected tender (NB: only the main contractor can accept the offer) on behalf of the employer after discussion.

Notify unsuccessful tenderers at once, but do not give tender figures until a decision to proceed with the successful tenderer has been reached. See specimen letters, Figs H.03, H.04.

Where there is a direct subcontractor/client agreement, and only if considered desirable in the particular circumstances, issue instructions concerning advance ordering of design works, materials, or fabrication. Do not do this before obtaining the client's agreement in writing. See specimen letters, Figs H.05, H.06.

After appointment of the main contractor, follow meticulously the procedures set out in the main contract for instructing the acceptance of the subcontract tender. Before issuing the instruction, check that the offer is still open for acceptance, and that the particulars on which the tender was based have not changed.

Fig H.01   **Specimen letter of preliminary invitation to tender**

It may be sufficient to make initial enquiries by telephone, but if a letter is preferable, this example may be used to approach:
- nominated contractors (JCT 80)
- named subcontractors (IFC 84)
- nominated suppliers (JCT 80).

The text should be adapted to suit the particular circumstances.

We are preparing a list of tenderers for specialist works and items in connection with this project.

(Under JCT 80, clause 35)
Tenders will be invited under JCT forms NSC/T and NSC/W and the standard conditions of subcontract NSC/C will apply.

(Under IFC 84, clause 3.3)
Tenders will be invited using JCT form NAM/T and the successful tenderer will be required to enter into agreement under form ESA/1 direct with the employer. Standard conditions of subcontract NAM/SC will apply.

(Under JCT 80, clause 19)
Tenderers who wish their names to be specified or listed as potential domestic subcontractors are asked to signify that they are able and willing at this stage to undertake the work and that they will cooperate in preparing a suitable description and measured items for inclusion in the main contract documents.

(Under JCT 80, clause 36)
Tenders will be invited using JCT form TNS/1 and the successful tenderer will be required to enter into Warranty TNS/2 direct with the employer.

(and)

If you wish to be included in our preliminary list of tenderers, you should reply by 12 noon on (date). You should also supply information about three recent commissions in which you have been involved, giving the names and addresses of the main contractor and architect in each case.

Fig H.02

Specimen letter of invitation to tender for domestic subcontract works

In the majority of cases, domestic subcontract works will be entirely a matter between the main contractor and his selected subcontractors. However, where the building contract makes provision for the architect to select subcontractors, who will nevertheless be domestic (eg under JCT IFC 84), this letter may be adapted to accompany the stipulated tender forms.

There may also be situations where the architect wishes to include the name of domestic subcontractors in main contract tender documents. If the building contract does not preclude this, the specimen letter of invitation might be appropriate.

We note that you wish to tender for the above works. We enclose:

. (three) copies of our Form of Tender
. one copy each of the 'numbered documents' (list them)
. an addressed envelope for the return of the Tender.

Please note that:

1 Drawings and details relating to the main contract may be inspected by arrangement with this office.

2 The site may be inspected by arrangement with (name) at (address).

3 Tendering procedures will follow the spirit of the NJCC Code of Procedure for Selective Tendering.

4 The Form of Tender should be completed fully and properly.

5 You may be required to enter into a design warranty agreement direct with the employer.

6 You should send three completed Forms of Tender in the enclosed envelope to reach this office not later than 12 noon on (date). Priced documents will be required later, if you are selected to execute the subcontract works, and upon acceptance by the main contractor.

7 Specialist drawings should be submitted to us for general inspection, but any failure on our part to detect inconsistencies or errors will not relieve you of responsibility.

Please confirm that you have received this letter and enclosures and that you are able to tender in accordance with these instructions.

Fig H.03

Specimen letter to unsuccessful tenderers for specialist subcontract works or supply items

This interim notification is not usually sent until after the successful tenderer has been selected.

```
We wish to inform you that the tenders were opened on (date) and
your price was not the lowest received. We will send you a list
of tenderers and prices in due course.

Thank you for tendering. Although your tender was not
successful, this will not prejudice your opportunities for
future work.
```

Fig H.04

Specimen letter notifying tendered prices for specialist subcontract works or supply items

```
Further to our letter of (date) we wish to inform you that
(name) have been appointed as specialist subcontractors (or
suppliers) for this work. The tenderers and tendered prices are
listed below. There is of course no correlation.
```

Fig H.05

Specimen advance order to named subcontractor

For use with IFC 84.

> On behalf of the employer we have approved your tender of (date)
> under form NAM/T and will issue an instruction to the contractor
> to accept this.
>
> In accordance with paragraphs 7.2 and 7.7 of Agreement ESA/1
> between you and the employer, we are authorised to issue the
> following instructions:
>
> (For example)
> . Please purchase the following materials:
> ... ...
> . Please fabricate the following components:
> ... ...
>
> and confirm in writing that you have put these matters in hand.
>
> Your rights concerning payment, and the right of the employer to
> the benefit of your work if the subcontract is not entered into,
> are covered in paragraph 7.2 of Agreement ESA/1.

Fig H.06

Specimen advance order to nominated subcontractor

For use with JCT 80.

> On behalf of the employer we have approved your tender of (date)
> under form NSC/T.
>
> Until the main contractor is appointed we are unable to issue a
> nomination instruction on form NSC/N. However, under Clause
> 2.2.1 of NSC/W, which became operative when we approved your
> tender, we are authorised to issue the following instructions:
>
> (For example)
> . Please design/prepare installation drawings in accordance
>   with the programme set out in your tender
> . Please order/fabricate the following items
>   ... ...
>
> and confirm in writing that you have put these matters in hand.
>
> Your rights concerning payment, and the right of the employer to
> the benefit of your work should nomination not proceed, are
> covered in Clause 2.2 of Agreement NSC/W.

List potential contractors

This will mean compiling a shortlist from scratch, or one drawn from a standing list. Among the points which should be considered in respect of the firms are:

- their financial standing;
- their reputation and relevant experience;
- their management structure and performance;
- their capacity;
- their competence and resources in respect of health and safety requirements.

Decide whether single or two stage tendering

Single stage operates on the assumption that full information is available to tenderers at the time of tendering. The tender figure is then the price for which the contractor offers to carry out and complete the works shown on the drawings and described in the contract bills/specification/schedules.

Two stage procedures allow the selection of the contractor by means of a first stage competitive tender based on 'pricing documents' relating to preliminary design information. There will then follow negotiations when the design is completed, and bills of quantities are priced on the basis of pricing provided in the first stage tender. This procedure is only suitable for large complex projects where there could be advantage in collaborating with the contractor during design stages.

Make preliminary enquiries

Send a preliminary invitation to tender, to selected potential contractors. This will enable contractors to decide whether they will tender, and allow them to programme tendering staff effort.

The letter of invitation should have attached to it a description of the project, relating to the form of contract it is intended to use. It is essential that full details are sent in this preliminary enquiry. See specimen letter and attachment, Fig H.07.

Invite tenders

Send formal letters to tenderers informing them of the date for issuing tender documents and the closing date for submission of tenders. Documents may be despatched by first class post or made available for collection if the number of documents is considerable.

A standard form of tender should be issued, and all tenderers clearly told that tenders will be submitted on exactly the same basis. Adequate time for tendering will be determined in relation to the size and complexity of the job. See specimen letters and specimen forms of tender, Figs H.08, H.09.

Any particular requirements of the client concerning, for example, guarantee bonds or a certificate of non-collusion should be clearly stated in the formal invitation. See specimen certificate, Fig H.10.

Deal with tenders

Tenders should be opened as soon as possible after the date for receipt, and strictly in accordance with the procedures agreed with the client. Qualified tenders should be rejected if it is considered that the qualification affords an unfair advantage, or the tenderer should be given an opportunity to withdraw the qualification.

The priced bills of quantities should be submitted at the same time as the tenders, but in separate sealed envelopes clearly marked with the tenderers' names. Bills from unsuccessful tenderers should be returned unopened.

Tenders under consideration should be referred to the Planning Supervisor to check adequacy of allocated resources in respect of health and safety requirements.

Examination of the priced bills of the lowest tenderer should be undertaken immediately by the QS. Errors will be dealt with according to which NJCC Code Alternative (Procedure 1 or 2) is to be applied. Any necessary reduction of the tender figure should be strictly to the NJCC Code.

Unsuccessful tenderers should be informed as quickly as possible, and once the contract has been let, every tenderer should be sent a list of firms who tendered (in alphabetical order) and a list of tender prices (in ascending order). It should not be possible to cross-reference the lists. See specimen letters, Fig H.11–13.

Fig H.07

Specimen letter of preliminary invitation to tender for main contract works

The purpose of this letter is to establish a list of potential main contractors. The Description of Project attached to it should relate to the form of contract it is intended to use.

The letter is based upon Appendix A.1 of the NJCC *Code of Procedure for Single Stage Selective Tendering 1994*.

We are preparing a list of tenderers for constructing the works (description attached) under the JCT standard form of building contract (eg JCT 80 or IFC 84 or MW 80). We draw your attention to the option clauses which will apply. Any amendments will be set out in the tender documents.

If you wish to be invited to tender on this basis you must agree to submit a bona fide tender in accordance with the NJCC Code of Procedure for Single Stage Selective Tendering 1994, and you must not divulge your tender price to any person or body before the time for submitting tenders. When the contract has been signed, we will send all those who tendered a list of the tenderers and prices.

Please reply to this letter by (date). Your inclusion in our preliminary list does not guarantee that you will receive a formal invitation to tender, nor will your opportunities for tendering for future work be prejudiced if you do not wish to tender this time.

(For JCT 80)

a   Job
b   Employer
c   Architect
d   Quantity surveyor
e   Consultants
f   Location of site (enclose site plan)
g   General description of the work
h   Approximate cost range £ .... to ....
i   Nominated subcontractors for major items
j   Form of contract (which edition, amendments, supplements)
k   Fluctuations (if applicable):
    Clause 38, 39, 40
    Percentage addition to clause 39.8 (if applicable)
l   Examination and correction of priced bills (section 6 of the Code):
    Alternative 1/Alternative 2 will apply
m   The contract is to be executed as a deed/simple contract
n   Anticipated date for possession is ....
o   Period for completing the works is ....
p   Approximate date for despatch of tender documents is ....
q   Tender period is .... weeks
r   Tender to remain open for .... weeks
s   Liquidated damages:
    anticipated value £ .... per ....
t   Details of bond/guarantee requirements
u   Particular conditions applying to this contract

Fig H.08   **Specimen letter of invitation to tender for main contract works using bills of quantities**

Suitable for use with JCT 80 and IFC 84 under the NJCC *Code of Procedure for Single Stage Selective Tendering*.

We note that you wish to tender for these works.

We enclose:
- two copies of the bill(s) of quantities
- two copies of the location drawings, component drawings, dimension drawings and information schedules
- two copies of the form of tender
- an addressed envelope in which to return the tender
- copies of relevant advance orders.

The completed form of tender, sealed in the envelope provided, should reach this office not later than 12 noon on (date).

Please note that:

1   Drawings and details may be inspected at (address).

2   The site may be inspected by arrangement with (name) at this office.

3   Tendering procedures will be in accordance with the NJCC Code of Procedure for Single Stage Selective Tendering 1994.

4   In respect of examination and adjustment of priced bill(s) under Section 6 of the Code, Alternative (1 or 2) will apply.

5   Any queries should be raised with (name) at this office.

6   The building owner reserves the right to accept any tender from those submitted or to refuse all.

Please confirm that you have received this letter and enclosures and that you are prepared to tender in accordance with these instructions.

Fig H 08
continued

Specimen form of tender for main contract works using bills of quantities

Suitable for use with JCT 80, IFC 84, either separately or attached to a letter of invitation.

We have read the conditions of contract and bills of quantities delivered to us and have examined the drawings referred to in them.

We offer to execute and complete in accordance with the conditions of contract the whole of the works described for the sum of £ .... (and in words) within (number of) weeks from the date of site possession.

We agree that if errors in pricing or arithmetic are discovered in the priced bills of quantities before this offer is accepted, they will be dealt with in accordance with Alternative (1 or 2) under Section 6 of the Code of Procedure for Single Stage Selective Tendering.

This tender remains open for consideration for (number of) days from the date fixed for submitting tenders.

We agree to provide a bond as required by the employer and name the following

1 ....

2 ....

(assurance/guarantee societies/banks) as sureties, who are willing to be bound jointly and severally by us to the employer in the sum of £ .... for the performance of this contract. The amount included in the tender sum to cover the provision of a bond is £ ....

Fig H.09

Specimen letter of invitation to tender for main contract works using drawings and specifications/schedules

Suitable for use with JCT 80, IFC 84 and MW 80 under the NJCC *Code of Procedure for Single Stage Selective Tendering.*

We note that you wish to tender for these works.

We enclose:

- two copies of the specifications/schedules and drawings and schedules
- two copies of the form of tender
- an addressed envelope in which to return the tender.

The completed form of tender, sealed in the envelope provided, should reach this office not later than 12 noon on (date).

Please note that:

1   Drawings and details may be inspected at (address).

2   The site may be inspected by arrangement with (name) at this office.

3   Tendering procedures will be in accordance with the NJCC Code of Procedure for Single Stage Selective Tendering 1994.

4   Any queries should be raised with (name) at this office.

5   The building owner reserves the right to accept any tender from those submitted or to refuse them all.

Please confirm that you have received this letter and enclosures and that you are prepared to tender in accordance with these instructions.

Fig H.09
continued

Specimen form of tender for main contract works using drawings and specifications/schedules

Suitable for use with JCT 80, IFC 84, MW 80, either separately or attached to letter of invitation.

We have read the conditions of contract and have examined the drawings, specifications and schedules which you have sent us.

We offer to execute and complete in accordance with the conditions of contract the whole of the works described for the sum of £ .... (and in words) within (number of) weeks from the date of site possession.

We enclose our schedule of rates (or contract sum analysis) giving a breakdown of our tender figure. We agree that if errors in pricing or arithmetic are discovered in the schedules etc before this offer is accepted, they will be dealt with on the basis of rules for the adjustment of priced bills of quantities as set out in Alternative (1 or 2) under Section 6 of the NJCC Code of Procedure for Single Stage Selective Tendering. This tender remains open for consideration for (number of) days from the date fixed for submitting tenders.

We agree to provide a bond as required by the employer and name the following

1 ....

2 ....

(assurance/guarantee societies/banks) as sureties, who are willing to be bound jointly and severally by us to the employer in the sum of £ .... for the performance of this contract. The amount included in the tender sum to cover the provision of a bond is £ ....

Fig H.10   **Specimen certificate of non-collusion**

For use as an appendix to any form of tender. The employer may have his own document for this purpose.

Recognising the principle that the essence of selective tendering is that the employer receives bona fide competitive tenders from all firms tendering, we certify that we will submit such tender, and that we will not fix or adjust the amount of the tender by or under or in accordance with any agreement or arrangement with any other person. We also certify that we have not done and we will not do at any time before the date for this tender to be submitted, any of the following acts:

1   Communicate to any person other than the person calling for our tender the amount or approximate amount of the proposed tender.

2   Enter into any agreement with or arrange for any other person to refrain from tendering, or indicate the amount of any tender to be submitted.

3   Reward, or promise to reward, any person for performing or causing any of the actions or effects described in 1 and 2 above.

In this certificate, the word 'person' includes any persons, bodies or associations, corporate or incorporate; and 'any agreement or arrangement' includes any such transaction, formal or informal, and whether legally binding or not.

Fig H.11　　　　**Specimen letter to contractor submitting most acceptable tender**

Where applicable the construction phase Health and Safety Plan of this tenderer should accompany priced documents and will be examined at the same time by the Planning Supervisor.

> We are pleased to inform you that your tender for these works was the most acceptable. The priced documents are now being examined by the quantity surveyor. Please send us priced documents as soon as possible.
>
> We will write to you again when the examination has been completed.

Fig H.12　　　　**Specimen letter to contractor submitting second most acceptable tender**

> The tenders were opened on (date). Yours was the second most acceptable.
>
> If the tender at present more acceptable than yours is found not to be satisfactory, you may be asked to stand by your tender and to submit bills of quantities.
>
> We will write to you again as soon as a decision has been reached, and in due course we will send you the full list of tenderers and tendered prices.

Fig H.13　　　　**Specimen letter to other unsuccessful tenderers**

> We regret to have to inform you that your tender was not successful. In due course we will send you a full list of tenderers and tendered prices.
>
> Thank you for tendering. Although you have been unsuccessful this time, this will not prejudice your opportunities of tendering for our work in the future.

Selective tendering:
Main contract – Design and build procurement

List potential contractors

This will mean compiling a preliminary shortlist of six to a maximum of twelve contractors. Among the points which should be considered in respect of the firms are:
- their financial standing;
- their reputation and relevant experience in design and build;
- their management structure and performance;
- their design capability and whether in-house or by unknown consultants;
- their capacity;
- their competence and resources in respect of health and safety requirements.

Make preliminary enquiries

Send a preliminary invitation to tender, to selected potential contractors. The letter of invitation should clearly state whether this is a single stage or two stage process, and the extent to which the contractor will be expected to design the works, and carry professional indemnity insurance.

The letter should have attached to it a description of the project, and information relating to planning requirements, eg whether the project is within a Conservation Area, likely to be affected by the Defective Premises Act 1972 etc.

Tenderers will also need to know the basis for awarding the contract, eg on price alone, and if not, the extent to which other considerations will be taken into account, such as design quality, maintenance or running costs.

Arrange interviews

After responses to the preliminary invitations have been received, the most suitable contractors should be interviewed. Matters to be raised might include:
- construction forms and methods favoured;
- time considered appropriate for tendering and mobilisation;
- design liability and insurance arrangements;
- professional and technical support available to the contractor;
- design and construction programme envisaged by the contractor.

The interviewing panel should include the client, the Planning Supervisor, and appropriate professional advisers.

Invite tenders

Send formal letters to selected tenderers either enclosing the tender documents in duplicate or informing them of the date for collection. The extent of these documents will depend on whether the tendering is single or two stage, but should include:
- a clear statement of the Employer's Requirements;
- additional information (eg drawings, specification notes) produced by the employer's consultants;
- details of the tendering requirements, type, format, and extent of information to be submitted.

A standard form of tender should be issued. Adequate time for tendering will depend on the size and complexity of the project, and whether this is a single or two stage submission.

Deal with tenders

Tenders should be opened as soon as possible after the date for receipt, and strictly in accordance with the procedures agreed with the client.

With a single stage procedure where price is stated to be the sole criterion, supporting design proposals and pricing documents should be submitted at the same time, but under separate cover.

With a two stage procedure the tender will also include an undertaking to enter into second stage negotiations on the basis of the first stage tender sum.

The examination of the Contractor's Proposals and pricing documents will be undertaken by the employer, the Planning Supervisor, and other professional advisers to establish that the Proposals are consistent with the Employer's Requirements.

Unsuccessful tenderers should be informed as quickly as possible, and all documents received should be treated as confidential and returned.

List potential contractors

This will mean compiling a preliminary list of a maximum of eight names, usually from an Approved List. Among the points to be considered in respect of the firms are:
- their financial standing and reputation;
- their recent experience in management or construction management contracts;
- their capacity;
- their competence and resources in respect of health and safety requirements.

It may sometimes be advisable to make some preliminary enquiries to obtain current necessary information before compiling the list.

Make preliminary enquiries

Send a preliminary invitation to tender to a small number of firms on the list. The letter of invitation should have attached to it a brief description of the project with project drawings if available, details of the tender procedures and method of evaluating tenders, and the anticipated duration of the project pre-construction and construction.

Arrange preliminary interviews

Because of the large or complex management nature of projects usually procured by this method, it might be necessary also to hold preliminary interviews at this stage. This will enable the employer to gain a better understanding of the philosophy and management structure offered by some of the potential firms, to an extent not obtainable solely through written enquiries.

Invite tenders

Send formal letters to selected tenderers. Tender documents should contain:
- clear conditions for the submission, so that all tenderers provide the same amount of information;
- proposed timescales pre-construction and construction;
- a clear indication of the assessment and interview procedures which will form part of the overall assessment.

Criteria to be satisfied will normally include:
- management service offered;
- key personnel for the project;
- financial: both in respect of fees and ability to manage costs;
- conditions of engagement;
- programmes;
- method statements.

Deal with tenders

Tenders should be opened as soon as possible after the date for receipt, and strictly in accordance with the procedure agreed with the client.

A detailed evaluation of each submission should be prepared. When the written submissions have undergone preliminary evaluation they can be assessed by the employer. It will then be necessary to interview each tenderer. This will enable them to explain their proposals in detail, clarify any points in the submission which need comment, and allow the employer to meet the key personnel which the tenderer proposes using. Further interviews may be necessary before a decision is reached.

Unsuccessful tenderers should be informed as soon as possible.

Project Planning J

J/1   **Activities**

J/2   **Actions**

J/3   **Stage summary**

J/4   **Watchpoints**

J/5   **Action checks**

Supplement

J/S1   Dealing with the contract documents

J/S2   Site inspectorate appointment and briefing

J/S3   Initial project team meeting

J/S4   Insurances check

Description

In the strict sense of the term, Project Planning is likely to be mainly the responsibility of the appointed contractor. However, an architect acting as the lead consultant can do much at this stage to see that the contract is properly set up from the outset.

Contract documents have to be prepared, and the agreement should be signed before work on site commences. There will need to be an exchange of information between architect and contractor, and confirmed agreement on procedures to be followed.

The client will enter into the building contract as the Employer, and the site given into the possession of the contractor so that work may proceed as programmed. The employer, contractor and relevant consultants will need to be advised on their respective responsibilities under the contract.

The contractor must have reasonable time to mobilise resources. Site inspectorate will need to be appointed and briefed. Arrangements should be made for the formal initial project team meeting, sometimes also referred to as the pre-start or pre-contract meeting.

Terminology

* The RIBA Plan of Work refers to Stage J Project Planning.

* RIBA standard appointing documents generally refer to Stage J Project Planning, although in some circumstances Stages J and K may be shown as linked.

* In Design and Build with an Employer Client, Stage J is often shown as Project Planning. With a Contractor Client, Stage J does not usually feature in the services which may be supplied by an architect.

* With Community Architecture projects, the scope of Stage J might be extended to include additional requirements for self-build groups, semi-skilled labour etc.

If coming new to the project at this Stage in the Plan of Work, carry out the relevant Pre-Agreement checks and note any General Procedures listed under earlier Stages which might apply.

If taking over a project on which others were engaged for earlier Plan of Work Stages, allow for familiarisation and checking of all usable material when agreeing fees and timetable with the client.

General procedures

- Establish the scope and content of Stage J. Put it into context, particularly if it follows Stages undertaken by others, or material produced is likely to be acted upon by others taking over subsequent Stages.

- Check with the Planning Supervisor that a construction phase Health and Safety Plan has been presented by the contractor and that there are no problems with health and safety requirements which might delay commencement of the construction phase.

- Agree with the client the extent of professional services for Stage J if not yet settled, and confirm in writing.

- Agree with the client the methods and levels of charging for Stage J if not yet settled, and confirm in writing.

- Assess the office resources needed for Stage J and ensure that they are adequate and available.

- Review the project quality plan, update and develop it as necessary.

- Check progress against the timetable for services regularly.

- Check expenditure against the office job cost allocation for Stage J.

- Report regularly to the client on fees and expenses incurred, and submit accounts at agreed intervals.

- Check that the client settles all accounts promptly.

- Set up accounts procedures for invoicing the appointed main contractor monthly for the cost of copies of drawings and documents additional to those stated in the contract, whether these involve prints or software.

Preliminary issues

Concerning the client

- Check that any necessary approvals and consents have been obtained and are on file. If any are still outstanding, explain to the client the consequences of starting on site prematurely.

- Check that the notice to Health and Safety Executive required by law has been deposited.

- Check that the client's Planning Supervisor has expressed satisfaction with the contractor's construction phase Health and Safety Plan, and that this is confirmed in writing.

· Check whether the client has confirmed the appointment of a clerk of works. If appointed, duties should be clearly defined and the person fully briefed.

· Remind the client that any insurances for which the client has accepted responsibility should have been taken out. Policies should be kept available for inspection by the contractor at all reasonable times.

· Discuss with the client the main contractor's master programme. Draw to the client's attention significant dates by which any further decisions or information will be needed, and by which any persons directly employed are programmed to start and finish.

Design and build · Check whether the client has confirmed the appointment of an Employer's Agent. The authority of this person should be clearly stated in writing, and the contractor should be informed. *(Employer Client)*

Team working

· Review post-tender situation. In the event of omission or substitution necessitating revisions to detail design, take appropriate action if authorised by the client. Alert the client to any additional costs, fees, or alterations to programme.

· Amend production information as necessary. Establish whether changes are to be reflected in the contract documents (which will then differ from tender documents) or whether amendments are to be the subject of immediate variations under an architect's instruction issued when the contract has been entered into.

· Check the effects of any amendments on specialist subcontract work and arrange for adjusted tenders if necessary.

· Record all amendments. Identify changes clearly on revised documents. Retain and file all original issues.

· Check scope of professional services agreed with the client, for continued presence of design team members as consultant members of the project team.

Costs

· Check with quantity surveyor, if appointed, contractor's Schedule of Rates and Contract Sum Analysis where relevant.

· Continue resource control procedures for office, and monitor expenditure against allocation of fee for Stage.

Preliminary issues
continued

Approvals/consents

· Check that all notices granting planning permission and approval under Building Regulations are to hand. Check that statutory approvals are still valid within time limits.

· Check that there are no other outstanding consents which could prevent the works being started on time.

· Check that Health and Safety Executive has been given particulars required by law under the CDM Regulations.

Contract

· Confirm to the client the responsibilities and obligations under the contract as Employer. Confirm the architect's role and duties as agent and contract administrator.

· Check that the insurance requirements of the contract have been met, and that the policies have been properly submitted for inspection.

· Remind the client of the obligation to honour certificates of payment in full and within the period stated in the contract.

· Remind the client that empowered instructions to the contractor can only be issued by way of an architect's instruction.

· Confirm the appointment of any clerk of works and brief site inspectorate.

· Prepare contract documents for signature. Send by registered/recorded post or deliver by hand. It is customary to send these first to the Contractor and then to the Employer.

· Check that copies of drawings and other documents are handed to the main contractor and clerk of works.

· Confirm dates for commencement and completion. Clarify any queries from the contractor. Establish and inspect contractor's programmes, confirm information schedules.

· Hold initial project team meeting with employer, main contractor, consultants, QS and clerk of works invited to attend.

· Arrange for handover of site and/or existing buildings, allowing the contractor exclusive possession or to the extent previously agreed.

· Inspect the contractor's method statements and master programme. Comment as appropriate.

· Compile directory of all involved at construction stages.

· Check that all unsuccessful tenderers have been properly notified.

Stage input

Information necessary during Stage H might include the following as relevant:

- Form of contract, with all necessary entries and Supplements, ready for completion by the parties.

- Contract documents, including drawings and Bills of Quantities/ Specification/Schedules of Work, incorporating any necessary adjustments, ready for issue.

- Published reliable commentaries or guides to assist with contract administration. Copies of relevant JCT Practice Notes and NJCC Guidance Notes.

- Administration forms published for use in contract administration, suitable for the particular contract to be used.

- Contractor's preliminary programme, and required method statements.

Stage output

Tangible results/material produced before the conclusion of Stage H might include the following as relevant:

- Bill of Reductions or similar document setting out agreed adjustments to the tender figure, if relevant, to arrive at an acceptable contract figure.

- Contract documents duly signed and Initialled as appropriate by Employer and Contractor as parties to the contract.

- Requisite sets of drawings, schedules and other documents for issue to the main contractor.

- Approved tenders and numbered documents in respect of specialist subcontractors for issue to main contractor.

- Health and Safety notice as required under CDM Regulations, to be deposited before work commences.

- Construction phase Health and Safety Plan by main contractor under the CDM Regulations.

- Requisite forms and documents for issue to the clerk of works.

* Post-tender cost reduction exercises usually mean additional work. Allow time for this.

* When preparing contract documents for signature or completion as a deed, check meticulously that entries are correct, and, if more than one copy, that they are identical.

* Check that tender documents and contract documents relate; if not, take formal steps to authorise changes.

* Carefully inspect the contractor's preliminary programme, particularly if it indicates dates by which critical information is required. Comment as appropriate but do not approve it.

* Call for the contractor's insurance policies for cover and renewal dates. Do not accept assurances or photocopies. Pass on to the employer for checking by his brokers or insurance advisers.

* Check for performance bonds if required. They should be obtained before the contract is signed – it may be impossible to obtain them after.

* Check that the Health and Safety notice has been deposited, and that the contractor has a construction phase Health and Safety Plan.

* Thoroughly brief site inspectorate who are under the direction of the architect. Give the clerk of works clear instructions on procedures and reporting.

* Check that all relevant contract documents are signed by the parties, and any agreed alterations initialled.

* As soon as the contract is let, provide the contractor with full documentation, including drawings and approved tenders for specialist subcontract work.

* Agree with the contractor an information schedule for issue of further necessary information, and determine whose responsibility this will be.

* When chairing the initial project team meeting, be fair, firm and pleasant. This is an opportunity to make relevant introductions and establish clear procedures.

* Check stationery stocks for correct and current contract administration forms.

		Tick if relevant	Initial if completed
01	Establish scope, content and context for Stage activities		
02	Check client's written instruction to proceed		
03	If coming new to project, refer to previous Stage checks		
04	Check appointing documents wrt services and fees		
05	Check client has settled all accounts submitted to date		
06	Review and develop project quality plan as necessary		
07	Check office resources wrt services, timetable, fee		
08	Revise drawings etc as necessary wrt accepted tender		
09	Check for discrepancies between tender and contract documents		
10	Check bonds, warranties required from contractor		
11	Inspect master programme prepared by contractor		
12	Check P/S has advised client on contractor's H & S Plan		
13	Confirm with client and P/S dates for construction phase		
14	Check with client and contractor that required insurance is effective		
15	Collate approved specialist tender documents for issue to contractor		
16	Collate contract information and drawings for issue to contractor		
17	Agree with contractor schedule for further necessary information		
18	Prepare contract documents for endorsement/signature		
19	Brief site inspectorate under architect's control		
20	Check necessary documents are available on site		
21	Check with contractor quality management proposals and procedures		
22	Check with contractor proposed site planning and accommodation		
23	Check with contractor arrangements for hoardings, site security etc		
24	Check that parties have properly signed contract documents		
25	Convene initial project meeting and issue agenda		
26	Chair initial project meeting and issue minutes		
27	Arrange formal handover of site to contractor		
28			
29			
30			

Supplement

J/S1   Dealing with the contract documents

J/S2   Site inspectorate appointment and briefing

J/S3   Initial project team meeting

J/S4   Insurances check

Dealing with the contract documents

Notifying all tenderers

A letter should be sent to the selected tenderer confirming the decision to accept his tender. This letter might state that a contract will not exist until the documents have been prepared and signed by the parties. If this is so, it is important to make sure that signing of the contract takes place before the date agreed for possession to avoid possible allegations of frustration.

As a general rule the formalities of the contract agreement should always be completed before work starts on site. However, where for some good reason there is insufficient time for the documents to be prepared before work has to commence, a letter accepting the selected tender may be sent. Once in the post, such a letter establishes a contractual relationship; it should therefore be sent by recorded delivery. The letter should inform the contractor that the employer is entering into the contract as intended and on the terms described in the tender documents, and that formal documents will follow by a specific date. There would then be an enforceable obligation to enter into a formal contract and the documents should be produced as quickly as possible. For a specimen letter, see Fig J.01.

Once the tender has been accepted, all tenderers should be informed of the tender prices submitted as recommended in the NJCC Codes of Procedure for Selective Tendering. For a specimen letter, see Fig J.02.

Completing the contract documents

Both parties should enter into a contract on the basis of a complete set of documents, each of which has been completed as necessary.

The Agreement between the employer and the contractor should be dated and reflect the correct titles and addresses of the parties. Normally the addresses will be those to which notices, instructions, certificates etc are to be sent. If either party wishes to have all contractual communications sent to a different address, this should be recorded in the contract documents.

The Recitals set out the facts on which the Agreement is based, and may start with the customary word 'Whereas'. The description of the intended works may be brief, but it should be clear and adequate. For example, 'constructing a factory and ancillary external works' or 'carrying out alterations to a bank' are clear enough for purposes of identification. The location of the site should also be conveyed precisely in a few words.

Often the name and address of the architect is to be entered in the Recitals and in an Article. The inclusion of the name in two places takes care of the possibility that the architect appointed under the building contract may not be the same person who was appointed to prepare the design.

The drawings which show the works need to be clearly identified. To avoid any risk of discrepancy, they should be those used for preparing the contract bills, specification or schedules of work as appropriate. Requirements might be met by including the site plan (taking care to show the physical boundaries of the works – particularly if they form part of a larger complex), general arrangement plans, sections and elevations, and any details necessary for the purposes of tendering. If the number of drawings is greater than can be described within the space available on the contract form, the words 'as in the attached list' may be inserted and a list headed 'Contract Drawings' be fixed securely to the page containing the relevant Recital. Drawings should be identified beyond all doubt by giving the correct number and issue affix (eg 261/32e). It might be worth using a rubber stamp to endorse each copy of contract drawings, bills, and any other written material which is to be incorporated as part of the contract. For example, 'This is one of the contract documents referred to in the contract between ... (Employer) and ... (Contractor) and signed hereunder (by both parties)'.

Where alternative contract provisions are to be deleted (an action not now required in the majority of current JCT forms of contract) this should be done clearly in the text of the document and should be initialled by the parties.

Whether options clauses are to apply or not should be clearly indicated in the Appendix.

Alterations to the text are possible, if that is what the parties want. They should be clearly indicated in the text of the document and initialled by the parties. They should be indicated at the time of tendering.

The conditions in standard forms of contract are often complex and interrelated. Even apparently innocuous alterations to a clause can affect or call into question other parts of the contract. Conditions should not be amended without considerable care and thought, and never without taking legal advice.

The NJCC has expressed concern over unnecessary amendments in Procedure Note 2. It is essential in the interests of good practice and economic building that amendments are kept to a minimum.

Most JCT forms of contract provide that the printed conditions of the contract take precedence over any typed or written words in other documents. Therefore any additional articles, conditions or amendments must not be left to the specification or to the preliminaries section of a bill of quantities, but must be properly incorporated in the actual articles or conditions.

Most JCT forms of contract have an Appendix. In the interests of accuracy, entries should be copied direct from the tender documents. Full information concerning matters to be included in the Appendix should be given at the time of tendering.

Where bills of quantities apply, the QS is required under the Standard Method of Measurement to recite the clause headings of the contract conditions to give tenderers an opportunity to price those conditions which may carry financial implications. Where there are no bills of quantities, a corresponding section in the specification or schedules of work should give such information for tenderers.

Signing the contract agreement

The form of building contract containing the Articles of Agreement is normally sent first to the contractor, accompanied by the drawings listed in the Recitals and the other contract documents as appropriate. Pencil in a cross to indicate where the contractor is to sign (usually in the lower set of spaces). Documents returned by the contractor should be examined carefully to see that they have been completed properly, as requested in the covering letter. For a specimen letter, see Fig J.03.

The documents should then be passed to the employer with a covering letter asking him to date the Articles. Documents returned from the employer should be examined carefully to see that they have been completed properly. For a specimen letter, see Fig J.04.

Signing confirmed

Instead of signing separately, the parties may agree to meet at some convenient place and complete the execution of the contract in each other's presence.

If the contract is to be executed as a simple contract, only the signatures of both parties are necessary. The signatures of witnesses – desirable, although not a legal necessity – confirm the existence of the agreement.

If the contract is to be executed as a deed, then appropriate wording should be used for the attestation clause. Special wording may be required depending on the Memorandum or Standing Orders of an authority or corporate body.

The manner of execution of the main contract does not necessarily mean that subcontracts or collateral agreements have to be similarly executed. However, thought should be given to this matter so as to avoid confusion and unnecessary complications and costs.

It is sometimes stated in the contract conditions who is to have custody of the original contract documents – usually the employer. The documents should be kept in a secure fireproof place. Copies of the contract documents should be suitably endorsed, for example, 'This is a certified copy of the Agreement dated ... between ... and ...' and signed by architect. A set is given to the contractor, and the architect would be wise to keep another complete set in the office safe.

Fig J.01 **Specimen letter to contractor notifying early start to the main contract works**

It is not good practice to commence the construction phase before the contract documents have been signed.

However, if circumstances are such that the client considers that the advantages of an early start outweigh the risks, adapt this letter according to the particular form of contract used, and the particular circumstances of the project.

Under no circumstances should construction work be started before the contractor has prepared a Health and Safety Plan which complies with the CDM Regulations.

We are pleased to inform you that our client intends to appoint you as Contractor on the basis of your tender dated .... in the sum of £ ...., and your submitted Health and Safety Plan.

The contract documents will be sent to you for signing not later than .... Meanwhile, will you please mobilise for site operations to commence on ...., when you will be given possession.

An initial project meeting will be held at this office on .... which will be attended by the Employer, Planning Supervisor, consultants and clerk of works. Please arrange to be represented by your key personnel.

You should immediately ensure that all insurances which are your responsibility under the building contract are effective, and original policy documents should be sent to us for our client to inspect. Please inform all specialist subcontractors and suppliers of the start date, and check that their insurance obligations have been discharged.

Please confirm in writing that you have put these matters in hand and send us the names of your personnel who will attend the initial project meeting.

Fig J.02   **Specimen letter notifying unsuccessful contractors**

We refer to our letter dated .... in which we confirmed
that your tender was not successful. We promised to send you the
full list of tenderers and tender prices, and we now list these
below. There is, of course, no correlation.

Tenderers
(in alphabetical order)

£ ....
  ....
  ....

Prices
(in descending order)

£ ....
  ....
  ....

Fig J.03   **Specimen covering letter to contractor with contract documents for signature**

These documents should be sent as soon as possible after notifying the contractor that his tender has been accepted.

Deliver by hand or send by Recorded Delivery.

Further to our letter of (date), we confirm that the employer wishes to enter into a contract with you and we enclose two sets of the contract documents. These comprise:

- Articles of Agreement and Conditions of Contract for completing as a simple contract (or as a deed)
- Contract drawings (nos.) and other contract documents (list) Bills of quantities in (number of) volumes Specification (or schedules) as appropriate.

Please complete the documents as follows:

- Sign where indicated and witness as necessary
- Initial all the alterations (indicated) in the Conditions to clauses (nos.)
- Sign every contract drawing and other contract drawing in the marked space
- Sign the specification (or schedules or bills of quantities) in the marked space.

Please return these documents to us as soon as possible, so that we can send them on to the employer for execution. We will provide you with one completed set in due course.

Fig J.04

Specimen covering letter to employer with contract documents for signature

Deliver by hand or send by Recorded Delivery.

The contractor has completed and returned to us the enclosed contract documents, which you should now sign. They comprise:

(List them, and repeat instructions for completion given in Fig J.03.)

Please return the documents to us after signature. We will date them and then send one set to the contractor and return the other set to you.

There are a few points of principle which we would like to bring to your attention at this stage.

1   Architect's responsibilities

As architects administering the contract we try to deal fairly in respect of the rights and duties of both parties, and we are responsible for issuing empowered instructions to the contractor. If you wish the contractor to be instructed about extra work or variations, please inform us so that we can discuss this with you. We will report to you regularly on progress and on the financial position.

2   Visits to site

The contractor will appreciate your interest in the progress of the works, but please ensure that only your authorised personnel visit the site and that this is arranged with the contractor beforehand. To safeguard your interests and to avoid any misunderstandings, the contractor has been specifically told not to accept instructions from anyone except us.

3   Payments

Payments will be authorised only on presentation of an architect's certificate. The amounts certified must be paid in full and within ...... days from the date issued. Prompt payment is essential to enable the contractor to discharge his obligations to subcontractors and suppliers and to complete on time.

If you would like any fuller explanations, please let us know.

On large works full time resident consultants (eg architects, engineers) might be needed to ensure conformity of materials, construction and quality, and also to liaise on the many activities upon which the full standards of the building's performance will depend. If such services are required, this must be clearly stated at tender stage.

On most large contracts a clerk of works is a full time and valuable presence. He must appreciate the extent of his powers, and generally his duties are to observe, inspect, check and report. His powers will be defined in the particular building contract, which may allow for him to be given considerable power by the project manager or Employer's Agent. Large schemes may justify specialist clerks of works, for example, for structural work or for services installations.

With JCT contracts the clerk of works operates under the direction of the architect and must be thoroughly conversant with the form of contract.

Clerk of works appointment

There are advantages in appointing a clerk of works before work commences on site. This arrangement may prove more difficult in the private sector, but the clerk of works can often comment from experience on construction matters and make a significant contribution to production information. Two weeks spent in the architect's office before going on site will allow a clerk of works to get to know the personnel and procedures associated with the project.

The appointment of a clerk of works for a particular project requires thoughtful preparation. It must be clearly established who is to be directly responsible for his appointment and payment, and ultimately for his performance. His duties will need to be carefully prescribed. Suitable candidates selected from a shortlist, or chosen on the basis of previous experience or personal recommendation, should be interviewed. A report can then be made to the client, and an appointment confirmed by letter, see Fig J.05.

Fig J.05

Specimen letter to newly appointed clerk of works

We are pleased to tell you that our client, (name), has confirmed your appointment on the terms agreed. These are itemised on the attached sheet/in the enclosed formal agreement.

Your duties will commence on (date), and you should report to the project architect, (name), with whom you will liaise throughout the project. He will supply you with project report forms, a daily diary, and a pad of Directions.

Will you please be sure to attend the initial project meeting on .... An agenda is attached. You will see that Clerk of Works' matters are included as item 4.

So that you can familiarise yourself with the project, we enclose a set of drawings, bills and specifications as issued to the Contractor, and a copy of the construction phase Health and Safety Plan.

We hope that you will enjoy working on this project. If you have any queries, please let us know.

Fig J.06   **Specimen form: Clerk of Works Project Report**

Clerk of Works **Project Report**   Report no: _____

Institute of
Clerks of Works

Project: _____   Ref. No: _____
Address: _____   Week ending: _____
_____

Architect/CA: _____
Main Contractor: _____   Contract start date: _____
Clerk of Works: _____   Contract completion date: _____
Tel: _____ Fax: _____   Progress against programme: _____

TRADES	Person in charge	Mon	Tue	Wed	Thu	Fri	Sat	Sun
(Man days)								
	Scaffolders							
Note	Groundworkers							
Main Contractor's Labour	Drivers and plant operators							
Return may be substituted	Steel fixers and concreters							
	Bricklayers and masons							
	Roofers: Finishes							
	Carpenters and joiners							
	Steel erectors							
	Window fixers							
	Plumbers							
	H & V engineers							
	Electricians							
	Lift engineers							
	Plasterers and screeders							
	Tilers: Wall and floor							
	Ceiling fixers							
	Floor finishers							
	Glaziers							
	Painters							
	Drainlayers							
	Statutory undertakers							
	Road pavers, Tarmac workers							
	Total man days							

WEATHER REPORT	Day	AM	°C	PM	°C	Man hours lost
	Monday					
	Tuesday					
	Wednesday					
	Thursday					
	Friday					
	Saturday					
	Sunday					
	Total man hours lost in week					
	TOTAL TO DATE					

Visitors to site	Name	Date
(including statutory inspectors)		

GENERAL COMMENTS _____
_____
_____
_____
_____

Fig J.06   *continued*

Site directions issued	No.	Item		Date

Delays

Defective work

Drawings/Information received on site

Drawings/Information requested on site

Plant/Materials delivered to site or removed

Health and safety matters

Working conditions on site

PROGRESS TO DATE

T = % Target
C = % Completed

	T	C		T	C		T	C
Preliminaries			Cladding/Curtain wall			Ceiling grid/Tiles		
Excavation			Windows – glazing			Decoration		
Shutter/Reinf			Joinery 1st fix			External works		
Concrete structure			Plastering			Hard/soft landscape		
Steel erection			Drylining/Partitions			Roadworks		
Main drainage m/h			Floor screeds			Mains: Gas		
Floor construction			Plumbing 1st fix			Mains: Electrical		
Floors suspended			Electrical 1st fix			Mains: Water		
Roof structure			H & V 1st fix			Mains: Telecoms		
Roof coverings			Wall/Floor tiles			Lifts		
Drainage fw. sw.			Plumbing 2nd fix			Alarm/Comp systems		
Brickwork external			Electrical 2nd fix			Defects/Handover		
Blockwork internal			H & V 2nd fix					

GENERAL REPORT   Summary of work proceeding

	Signed	(Clerk of Works)	Date

Complete as appropriate	**Enclosures**	**Distribution**	
	☐ Main Contractor's Labour Return	☐ Architect/CA	☐
	☐ Site Directions	☐	☐
	☐ Reports	☐	☐

Office action

The *Clerk of Works Manual* (Third Edition 1994, RIBA Publications) is a useful source of information. It sets out standard terms of appointment, defines duties and responsibilities, lists the documents which the clerk of works should maintain and offers a range of forms which might assist both the clerk of works and the architect.

Clerk of works briefing

The architect may decide to hold a special meeting to brief the site inspectorate. The architect should describe the project fully, the methods of construction to be used, and the programme of work. More particularly for the clerk of works, the architect should:
- explain routines and procedures to be followed;
- stress the need for work to conform with drawings and instructions, and that materials and workmanship must meet the required standards;
- stress the need to ensure that the latest editions of the relevant British Standards and Codes of Practice are available for reference on site.

As part of the briefing process, the clerk of works might expect to be supplied with the following:
- form of building contract, incorporating any supplements or amendments;
- contract bills of quantities (unpriced) and/or specification;
- contract drawings and schedules;
- 'numbered documents' or other information relating to specialist subcontracts;
- the employer's health and safety policy requirements and the construction phase Health and Safety Plan;
- site diary;
- reports forms;
- quality management plan, contractor's method statement, quality control checklists, verification forms etc.

The clerk of works should also be briefed about his responsibilities and extent of authority in connection with:
- hours of working and notification of additional hours;
- daily labour returns and method of submitting them;
- method of recording time lost in site working;
- signing of authorised daywork vouchers;
- samples of materials;
- testing of samples;
- storage of materials;
- notification of work to be covered up after inspection;
- general procedures for inspection and recording.

Clerk of works reporting

The duties of a clerk of works are to observe, inspect, check and report. A site diary is for recording day-to-day events. There is also a need to provide the architect with periodic reports to record progress on site, usually on a weekly basis. Printed forms will be provided for the clerk of works to complete and sign. The Institute of Clerks of Works publishes a Project Report Form which will be suitable for most situations, see Fig J.06.

This meeting, often referred to as the pre-contract or pre-start meeting, is crucial.

The site inspectorate may have already been briefed at separate meetings, or the briefing could form part of the initial project team meeting. At the meeting, all personnel will be introduced and lines of communication can be unequivocally identified and defined. This is the first opportunity for all the project team to meet and for effective working arrangements to be established.

It is essential for the person identified as the contract administrator to know the full range of contractual requirements of the project, and to be alert to potentially difficult areas. As chairman of the meeting, this person must establish mutual confidence and see that different viewpoints are aired and accommodated before the project gets under way.

The business of the meeting is likely to cover a wide range of topics, and it is important to start with a clear agenda and stick to it. For a specimen agenda, see Fig J.07.

Agenda items at initial project team meeting

Introductions

- Introduce the representatives who will regularly attend progress meetings and clarify their roles and responsibilities. The client, contractor and consultants may wish to introduce themselves.
- Briefly describe the project and its priorities and objectives, and any separate contract which may be relevant (preliminary, client's own contractors etc).
- Indicate any specialists appointed by the client, eg for quality control, commissioning, for this contract.

Contract

- Describe the present position with regard to preparation and signature of documents.
- Hand over any outstanding production information, including nomination instructions, variation instructions. Review situation for issuing other important information.
- Request that insurance documents be available for inspection immediately; remind the contractor to check specialist subcontractors' indemnities. Check if further instructions are needed for special cover. Clarify what standards, quality of work and management are required during the execution of the works.

Contractor's matters

- Check that the contractor's master programme is in the form required and that it satisfactorily accommodates the specialist subcontractors. It must:
  - contain adequate separate work elements to measure their progress and integration with services installations;
  - allocate specific dates for specialist subcontract works, including supply of information, site operations, testing and commissioning;
  - accommodate public utilities etc.

- The contractor's schedule of information required from architect/consultants must relate to his works programme and must be kept up to date.

Contractor's matters
continued

- Include in the schedule information, data, drawings etc to be supplied by the contractor/specialist subcontractors to the architect/consultants. It must be regularly reviewed.
- Review in detail the particular provisions in the contract concerning site organisation, facilities, restrictions, services etc to ensure that no queries remain outstanding.
- Quality control is the contractor's responsibility. Remind him about his duties to supervise, your duties to inspect, and the clerk of works'/site inspectorate's duties in connection with the works.

- Numerous other matters may need special coverage, eg:
  - immediate action over specialist subcontractors and suppliers;
  - review position on outstanding matters;
  - handover responsibility for advance orders already placed;
  - emphasise that drawings, data etc received from contractor or specialist subcontractors will be inspected by architect/consultants (*not* approved), and will remain the responsibility of the originator;
  - review outstanding requirements for information to or from the contractor in connection with specialist works;
  - clarify that the contractor is responsible for coordinating performance of specialist works and for their workmanship and materials, for providing specialists with working facilities, and for coordinating site dimensions and tolerances.
- The contractor must also provide for competent testing and commissioning of services as set out in the contract documents. He should be reminded that the time allocated for commissioning is not a contingency period for the main contract works.
- The contractor must obtain the architect's written consent before subletting any work.

Clerk of works' matters

- Clarify that architect's inspections are periodic visits to meet the contractor's supervisory staff, plus spot visits.
- Explain the supportive nature of the clerk of works' role and the need for cooperation to enable him to carry out his duties.
- Remind the contractor that he must provide the clerk of works with adequate facilities and access, together with information about site staff, equipment, and operations for his weekly reports to the architect.
- Confirm procedures for checking quality control, eg through:
  - certificates, vouchers etc as required;
  - sample material to be submitted;
  - samples of workmanship to be submitted prior to work commencing;
  - test procedures set out in the bills of quantities;
  - adequate protection and storage;
  - visits to suppliers'/manufacturers' works.

Consultants' matters

- Emphasise that consultants will liaise with specialist subcontractors only through the contractor. Instructions are to be issued only by the architect. The contractor must fulfill his management responsibility for the performance of the specialist subcontractors.
- Establish working arrangements for specialists' drawings and data for evaluation (especially services) to suitable timetables. Aim to agree procedures which will speed up the process; this sector of work frequently causes serious delay or disruption.

Quantity surveyor's matters

- Agree procedures for valuations; these may have to meet particular dates set by the client to ensure that certificates can be honoured.
- Clarify:
  - that dayworks will only be accepted on written instructions;
  - that daywork sheets are required within a stated number of days of work being carried out;
  - tax procedures concerning VAT and 'contractor' status;
  - that the contractor should only order from drawings and specifications, not from the bills of quantities.

Communications and procedures

- The supply and flow of information will depend upon programmes being established at the start (see item 3) and subsequently if:
  - there is regular monitoring of the information schedules;
  - requests for further information are made specifically in writing, not by telephone;
  - the architect responds quickly to queries;
  - technical queries are raised with the clerk of works (if appointed) in the first instance;
  - policy queries are directed to the architect;
  - discrepancies are referred to the architect for resolution, not the clerk of works or contractor.
- On receiving instructions, check for discrepancies with existing documents; check that documents being used are current.
- Information to or from specialist subcontractors or suppliers must be via the contractor.
- All information issued by the architect is to be via the appropriate forms, certificates, notifications etc. The contractor should be encouraged to use standard formats and classifications.
- All forms must show the distribution intended; agree numbers of copies of drawings and instructions required by all recipients.
- Clarify that no instructions from the client or consultants can be accepted by the contractor or any subcontractor; only empowered written instructions by the architect are valid and all oral instructions must be confirmed in writing. Explain the relevant procedures under the contract. The contractor should promptly notify the architect of any written confirmations outstanding.
- Procedures for notices, applications, or claims of any kind are to be strictly in accordance with the terms of the contract; all such events should be raised immediately the relevant conditions occur or become evident.

Meetings

- Always issue an agenda beforehand for all architect's meetings and circulate minutes promptly. Agree with the contractor and consultants that:
  - minutes are to be taken as directions for action only where specifically stated and agreed;
  - any dissent is to be notified with 7 days;
  - all persons attending will have authority to act.
- Agree copies and distribution required.
- See also Stage K–L for a summary of the various types of meeting for project administration, and the specimen agenda for the architect's site progress meetings, Fig KL.02. See Stage K–L for advice about site inspections.

Fig J.07   **Specimen agenda for initial project meeting**

1 **Introductions**
    Appointments, personnel
    Roles and responsibilities
    Project description

2 **Contract**
    Priorities
    Handover of production information
    Commencement and completion dates
    Insurances
    Bond (if applicable)
    Standards and quality

3 **Contractor's matters**
    Possession
    Programme
    Health and Safety File and Plan
    Site organisation, facilities and planning
    Security
    Site restrictions
    Contractor's quality control policy and procedures
    Subcontractors and suppliers
    Statutory undertakers
    Overhead and underground services
    Temporary services
    Signboards

4 **Clerk of works' matters**
    Roles and duties
    Facilities
    Liaison
    Dayworks

5 **Consultants' matters**
    Structural
    Mechanical
    Electrical
    Others

6 **Quantity surveyor's matters**
    Adjustments to tender figures
    Valuation procedures
    Remeasurement
    VAT

7 **Communications and procedures**
    Information requirements
    Distribution of information
    Valid instructions
    Lines of communication
    Dealing with queries
    Building Control notices

8 **Meetings**
    Pattern and proceedings
    Status of minutes
    Distribution of minutes

Insurance in the context of building construction is a highly specialised area, but one of great importance for the contract administrator. Certain insurance obligations arise from legislation, but the building contract will usually contain specific requirements concerning insurance cover against injury or damage caused during the works.

These requirements will have been discussed with the client, and the implications fully explained, prior to tender stage. The cost of insurance premiums will have been taken into account by the tenderers. Responsibility for the required cover, whether taken out by the contractor or the employer, will have been established.

Whereas the checking of policy wording is a matter for insurance experts advising either the contractor or the employer as relevant, it is for the contract administrator to check that the obligations to take out cover have been complied with.

An insurances check is necessary before any work on site is commenced. Although most contractors carry an annual policy, endorsements and some cover can take time to arrange. It may be that in some circumstances it proves impossible to obtain the cover stated, in which case it will be for the parties to the contract to decide the arrangements to apply.

Specialist subcontractors are sometimes mainly responsible for damage which occurs, and such an eventuality must be properly covered. The employer pays the cost of insurance in the end, and it is important to avoid the risk of double insurance. Cover must be adequate, and any figures entered in the building contract should be realistic after taking expert advice on the particular circumstances. The mere repetition of some previously quoted sum is a recipe for disaster.

At project planning stage it is vital to ensure that the required insurances are in place before work commences.

For a schedule listing the insurance options included in commonly used JCT contracts (MW 80, IFC 84, JCT 80), see Fig J.08.

Fig J.08   **Schedule of insurance responsibilities under JCT standard forms**

MW 80	IFC 84	JCT 80	Cover	Action
			Insurance against injury to persons and damage to property	
6·1 6·2	6·1·1 6·1·2	21·1·1	Insurance to cover the liability of the contractor or subcontractor against injury to persons and property due to the extent of the contractor's negligence. Cover for any one occurrence or series of occurrences arising out of one event, for not less than the sum stated (either in the relevant clause or the Appendix to the contract).	*Employer* None needed. *Contractor* Arrange immediately for adequate cover. (Figure in contract is only the *minimum* required.) Send documentary evidence to architect for inspection by employer.
			Special insurance against damage to property other than the works	
NA	6·2·4	21·2·1	Insurance in respect of expense, liability, loss, claim or proceedings which the employer may incur by reason of damage to property other than the works and not due to negligence by the contractor or a subcontractor. The Appendix shows that it may be required. Cover in the amount shown in the Appendix for any one occurrence or series of occurrences arising out of any one event.	*Employer* Instruct contractor through architect. Approve insurance. *Contractor* Arrange immediately on receipt of architect's instructions the joint names cover required (usually necessary right from start of site operations). Send documentary evidence to architect for inspection by employer.
			Insurance of the works by contractor against all risks (new buildings)	
NA	6·3A	22A	All risks insurance of the works etc, in joint names, for full reinstatement value (to include professional fees).	*Employer* Approve insurers. *Contractor* Arrange immediately for adequate cover. Supply annual renewal date if applicable. Send documentary evidence to architect for inspection by employer.
			Insurance of the works by contractor against fire etc (new works)	
6·3A	NA	NA	Insurance of the works in joint names against loss and damage by fire etc for full reinstatement value (to include professional fees).	*Employer* None needed. *Contractor* Arrange immediately for adequate cover. Produce documentary evidence as required by employer.

Fig J.08			*continued*		

MW 80	IFC 84	JCT 80	Cover		Action
			Insurance of the works by employer against all risks (new buildings)		
NA	6·3B	22B	All risks insurance of the works in joint names, for full reinstatement value (to include professional fees).		*Employer* Arrange immediately for adequate cover. (Note that cost of reinstatement is deemed a variation and is to be valued as such. Employer will bear excess and shortfall.) Produce documentary evidence as required by contractor. *Contractor* None needed.
			Insurance of the works against specified perils (existing structures)		
NA	6·3C	22C	Insurance of existing structures and contents in joint names against specified perils for full cost of reinstatement, repair or replacement.		*Employer* Arrange immediately for adequate cover (see previous action note). *Contractor* None needed.
			Insurance of the works against fire etc (existing structures)		
6·3B	NA	NA	Insurance in joint names against loss and damage by fire etc of existing structures and contents, and new works.		*Employer* Arrange immediately for adequate cover (see previous action note). *Contractor* None needed.
			Insurance against employer's loss of liquidated damages		
NA	6·3D	22D	Insurance to cover employer's loss of liquidated damages, where Appendix shows that it may be required.		*Employer* Instruct contractor through architect to obtain a quotation. Instruct on acceptance of quotation. *Contractor* When instructed by architect, obtain quotations. Arrange cover immediately if instructed to accept quotation. Send documentary evidence to architect for deposit with employer.

Operations on Site and Completion K-L

K–L/1   **Activities**

K–L/2   **Actions**

K–L/3   **Stage summary**

K–L/4   **Watchpoints**

K–L/5   **Action checks**

Supplement

K–L/S1   Keeping the client informed

K–L/S2   Site meetings

K–L/S3   Site inspections

K–L/S4   Issuing instructions

K–L/S5   Dealing with claims

K–L/S6   Issuing certificates

K–L/S7   Preparing for handover

K–L/S8   Post-completion

Description

The extent of the architect's involvement as the person nominated to administer the building contract will depend on both the terms of the contract for professional services and the wording of the building contract.

The parties to the building contract have brought into being obligations which are entirely of their own choosing and which do not directly devolve on to others. The conditions to which they have agreed bind only themselves. Where the conditions require the appointment of a contract administrator, his authority will be defined in the contract.

With traditional procurement, the contractor undertakes to:
- carry out and complete the works in accordance with the contract;
- proceed regularly and diligently;
- complete by the agreed completion date;
- comply with instructions empowered by the contract.

With traditional procurement, the client or employer undertakes to:
- give the contractor possession in order to carry out the work;
- ensure all necessary information is made available to the contractor;
- appoint a contract administrator;
- pay all amounts properly certified.

With traditional procurement, the contract administrator:
- issues necessary information to the contractor;
- issues instructions empowered or required by the contract;
- issues certificates as required by the contract;
- does not exceed the authority given by the contract;
- acts in a fair and reasonable manner where impartial judgement is required by the contract.

With design and build procurement, the architect's direct involvement in contract administration will probably be nil. Where acting for an Employer Client, consultancy advice might be needed, or under rare circumstances an architect might be appointed as Employer's Agent. Where acting for a Contractor Client, any involvement will not go beyond giving consultancy advice. There is no role for the impartial contract administrator with design and build procurement.

With management procurement, there is usually the need for an independent contract administrator, whose duties will normally include the issue of necessary information and instructions, and the issue of certificates. The obligations of the contractor will differ from those under traditional procurement, and be fully described in the contract.

Terminology

∗ The RIBA Plan of Work refers separately to Stage K Operations on Site, and Stage L Completion.

∗ RIBA standard appointing documents generally refer to Stages K–L Operations on Site and Completion, but in some circumstances K is linked to J, and Stage L is referred to as Defects Liability Period and final account.

∗ In Design and Build with either an Employer Client or a Contractor Client, Stage K–L is identified as Operations on Site.

If coming new to the project at this Stage in the Plan of Work, carry out the relevant Pre-Agreement checks and note any General Procedures listed under earlier Stages which might apply.

If taking over a project on which others were engaged for earlier Plan of Work Stages, allow for familiarisation and checking of all usable material when agreeing fees and timetable with the client.

General procedures

- Establish the scope and content of Stages K–L. Put it into context, particularly if it follows Stages undertaken by others.

- Agree with the client the extent of professional services for Stages K–L if not yet settled, and confirm in writing.

- Agree with the client the methods and levels of charging for Stages K–L if not yet settled, and confirm in writing.

- Assess the office resources needed for Stages K–L and ensure that they are adequate and available.

- Review the project quality plan, update and develop it as necessary.

- Check progress against the timetable for services regularly.

- Check expenditure against the office job cost allocation for Stages K–L.

- Report regularly to the client on fees and expenses incurred, and submit accounts at agreed intervals.

- Check that the client settles all accounts promptly.

- Maintain accounts procedures for invoicing the contractor for copies of additional drawings and documents.

- Set up procedures to issue certificates and fee accounts regularly. Issue final certificate and final fee account only when all obligations are complete.

Preliminary issues

Concerning the client

- Check with the client that the contract documents have been completed and signed as a simple contract or a deed as applicable.

- Check that the site or existing buildings have been given into the possession of the appointed contractor for the duration of the works.

- Remind the client of his statutory obligations under the CDM Regulations relating to the role of the Planning Supervisor and the competence of the Principal Contractor and other contractors' performance in health and safety matters.

- Advise the client of his obligations as Employer under the building contract and of the role and duties of the architect in administering the building contract.

· Remind the client that all instructions to the main contractor must be channelled through the architect.

· Remind the client of his obligations as Employer under the building contract to honour monetary certificates within the periods stated in the contract.

· Discuss with the client the need to appoint maintenance staff in time to attend the commissioning of the project, and to enter into maintenance agreements if relevant.

· Discuss with the client requirements for 'as built' information and maintenance manuals.

· Advise the client on the need to take over insurance of the completed works at the appropriate time.

· Remind the client of the requirement for a Health and Safety File to be deposited in a safe place at the completion of the project.

Team working

· Maintain liaison during construction stages through architect's progress meetings.

· Confirm that all instructions concerning specialist subcontractors or suppliers are to be channelled through the architect. If acceptable, they will be included under an architect's instruction issued to the main contractor.

· Confirm that consultants are to supply relevant information for the preparation of operating instructions, maintenance manuals, record drawings of installation etc.

· Confirm that consultants are to pass relevant information to the Planning Supervisor for inclusion in the Health and Safety File.

· Confirm that consultants are to carry out detailed inspection of specialist work and report to the architect. If authorised, they should also attend commissioning, testing and witnessing, and report.

Costs

· Keep the client regularly updated on the financial position as the works proceed. Adopt the client's own procedure/format if required.

· Liaise with QS to monitor costs arising from architect's instructions, and for forecasting monthly reports.

· Provide the client with estimates of costs arising from architect's instructions, including variations.

· Notify QS of any work against which monies must be withheld or where 'an appropriate deduction' is to be made from the contract sum.

Actions

Preliminary issues
continued

- Liaise generally with QS over remeasurement, valuations, and the issue of monetary certificates.

- Deal with applications for reimbursement of direct loss and/or expense fairly and promptly.

- Advise the client about any extra fees which might arise in connection with architect's instructions.

- Continue resource control procedures for office, and monitor expenditure against allocation of fee for Stage.

- Report to the client on cost matters at agreed intervals.

Inspections/tests

- Visit the site as appropriate, whether for periodic checks, predictive checks or spot checks, to observe and comment on the contractor's site supervision and examples of his work.

- Check that work is being executed generally in accordance with the provisions of the building contract, in a proper and workmanlike manner and in accordance with the Health and Safety Plan. Inspect the contractor's progress measured against the master programme, and generally inspect goods and materials delivered to the site.

- Prepare an inspection plan which identifies when visits should be made, and when checks can be made on tests which the contractor is obliged to make under the contract.

- Inform the client in advance if more frequent visits are required than those allowed for in the Agreement and which would incur additional expenditure.

- Check the contractor's quality management performance measured against the plan submitted in the contractor's method statement.

- Brief site inspection staff, including the clerk of works if appointed, about their duties and the procedures to be followed.

- Keep methodical records of all site visits and results of all tests witnessed or reported.

Contract

- Provide the contractor with copies of contract documents as required under the contract.

- Meet the contractor on site to note setting out, including boundaries, fencing and hoardings, site huts, amenities and welfare arrangements, protective measures, spoil heaps etc to establish compliance with contractor's method statements and contract requirements.

- Administer the terms of the contract fairly and impartially as between the parties, or in the case of non-traditional contracts, strictly in accordance with the contract provisions.

· Issue architect's instructions, discretionary or obligatory as empowered under the contract, and strictly in accordance with the contract provisions.

· Convene architect's progress meetings, and make site visits as provided for in the Agreement with the client.

· Attend contractor's progress meetings when invited.

· Provide additional necessary information to the contractor as required under the contract provisions.

· Request vouchers from the contractor as empowered under the contract.

· Issue certificates as empowered and required in accordance with the contract procedures.

· Liaise with the clerk of works and consultants throughout the construction stages.

· Liaise with the QS over remeasurement, valuations, and applications for loss and/or expense throughout the construction stages.

· Respond fairly and reasonably to notices and applications by the contractor, as required under the contract provisions.

· Maintain 'as built' records or drawings, as required under the contract provisions and pass relevant information to the Planning Supervisor for possible incorporation in the Health and Safety File.

· Check that the clerk of works and consultants maintain adequate records and pass relevant information to the Planning Supervisor for possible incorporation in the Health and Safety File.

· Advise the client, should partial possession be desired, about the contractual implications and procedures.

· Obtain contractor's forecast date for practical completion and advise the client of the procedures.

· Initiate pre-completion checks on the works with the clerk of works and compile list of outstanding items.

· Remind the client of the desirability of appointing maintenance staff in time to attend contractor's commissioning, and if relevant, client witnessing.

· Check that commissioning, testing and witnessing of engineering services is carried out according to the provisions of the contract.

· Hold formal handover meeting.

· Check that information relating to the Health and Safety File, maintenance manuals and operating instructions, is complete and ready for handing over to the Planning Supervisor.

· Issue certificate of practical completion in accordance with the provisions of the contract.

Preliminary issues
continued

· Prepare list or schedule of defects to be made good at the end of the defects liability period, in accordance with the provisions of the contract. Issue to the contractor within the period stated in the contract.

· Carry out final inspection of the works and issue certificate of making good defects.

· Issue final certificate, but only when all the requirements of the contract provisions have been satisfied.

Stage input

Information necessary during Stages K–L might include the following as relevant:

- Coordinated production information: drawings, drawn schedules, priced Bills of Quantities/Specification/Schedules of Work.

- Contractor's Rates or Contract Sum Analysis if appropriate, and/or priced Bills of Quantities/Specification/Schedules of Work.

- Specialists' tenders and 'numbered documents' ready for nomination instruction to be issued.

- Contractor's Master Programme.

- Copies of the construction phase Health and Safety Plan developed by the contractor and certified by the Planning Supervisor.

- Copies of method statements prepared by the contractor as required in the contract conditions.

- Schedule from contractor indicating what further information is needed from the architect and by when.

- Verification by the contractor, if applicable, that all necessary information has been supplied, and accepting that any further drawings will be his own responcibility.

- Sets of administration forms appropriate for the form of contract being used.

Stage output

Tangible results/material produced before the conclusion of Stages K–L might include the following as relevant:

- Information (drawn and written), decisions and instructions (obligatory or discretionary), as necessary for the contractor to perform his obligations under the contract, issued during the progress of the works.

- Valuations (on minor works) and certificates (monetary and otherwise), issued in accordance with the contract, during the progress of the works.

- Records of all correspondence, instructions and certificates, and 'state of the art' documents, whether from manufacturers or other sources, which should be retained in case there are later disputes.

- 'As built' drawings, manuals or other maintenance information required under the contract.

- Health and Safety File information, as required under the CDM Regulations.

- Final certificate, to be issued only when all outstanding contractual obligations are performed.

- Programmes for maintenance, if required.

* Acquire a good knowledge and understanding of all the contract documents.

* Administer the contract strictly in accordance with the procedural rules and the conditions.

* All instructions to the contractor should be in writing. They should be issued on an Architect's Instruction form (not via correspondence or site meeting minutes). Check that instructions are empowered, and the wording concise and unambiguous.

* Issue instructions or confirm oral instructions as soon as necessary to avoid difficulties and to ensure that cost appraisals are realistic.

* Take steps to ensure that there is no reasonably necessary information outstanding, general or specific. Watch the contractor's programme and progress for indicated dates and signs.

* Be methodical with regard to site visits. It helps to prepare checklists relating to the stage of the work. Allow adequate time on site to carry out checks properly. Make careful notes and compile a systematic record of visits.

* Keep accurate minutes of meetings and record discussions methodically. In assessing subsequent claims or allegations, these records may prove invaluable and more than justify the effort needed to maintain them.

* Variations should be pre-priced if possible; otherwise the likely full implications should be estimated and agreed before action is taken.

* Report regularly to the client on progress, and provide regular financial reports.

* Deal with all claims promptly, fairly and firmly, and within any stipulated scale. It may be that negotiation is the best way forward, but do not exceed your authority. Do not be overawed by the volume of documents sometimes presented by claims consultants. Quantity does not equate with the validity of a case.

* If possible, nominated or named subcontractors should be appointed at the commencement of the contract, always strictly in accordance with stipulated procedures. Note the subcontract dates for compatibility with the main contractor's programme.

* Be punctilious about valuations and certificates for payment. Notify the contractor in writing of any work not properly carried out, with a copy to the QS, so that such work is not included in any valuation.

* When completion is near, make sure that the contractor is fully aware that commissioning must be completed and operating manuals available before the building is handed over.

* Start a system for listing outstanding items of work to monitor progress towards completion. Finishing a contract often needs a special effort from the contractor, and pressure from the architect.

* Where the contract calls for record drawings or as built information, get these together in good time. The clerk of works can often help.

* Remind the client of his responsibility for the building in terms of insurance, security and maintenance in good time.

* Make sure that operating manuals have been properly checked and are ready by the time of handover.

* Cooperate with the Planning Supervisor, who will want to make sure that the Health and Safety File has been compiled and is ready at the time of handover.

* Certify practical completion only when, in your opinion, this state has been attained.

* Do not certify completion of the making good of defects or issue a final certificate until you are sure that there are no matters still outstanding.

		Tick if relevant	Initial if completed
01	Establish scope, content and context for Stage activities		
02	Check client's written instruction to proceed		
03	If coming new to project, refer to previous Stage checks		
04	Check appointing documents wrt services and fees		
05	Check client has settled all accounts submitted to date		
06	Review and develop project quality plan as necessary		
07	Check office resources wrt services, timetable, fee		
08	Issue documents to contractor as required under contract		
09	Issue instructions wrt prov. sums, appt. of specialist S/Cs etc		
10	Confirm with client and QS procedures for valuation, certification		
11	Issue AIs, mandatory or discretionary, as empowered by the contract		
12	Confirm with clerk of works procedures for reporting		
13	Confirm programme, procedures for architect's site progress meetings		
14	Confirm programme, procedures for architect's site visits		
15	Check designers' cooperation with P/S		
16	Check contractor's compliance with quality management procedures		
17	Issue certificates as required by contract		
18	Review H & S File information at regular intervals		
19	Check with client and contractor arrangements for commissioning, testing		
20	Check with contractor readiness for practical completion, advise client		
21	Explain to client implications of practical completion		
22	Check availability of operational information, keys etc for handover		
23	Inspect, and certify practical completion if appropriate		
24	Issue schedule of defects at end of defects liability period		
25	Check for application of CDM Regs to remedial works and report		
26	Inspect making good of defects and certify accordingly		
27	Check with P/S that updated H & S File is given to client		
28	Issue final certificate for remainder of adjusted contract sum		
29			
30			

Supplement

K–L/S1   **Keeping the client informed**

K–L/S2   **Site meetings**

K–L/S3   **Site inspections**

K–L/S4   **Issuing instructions**

K–L/S5   **Dealing with claims**

K–L/S6   **Issuing certificates**

K–L/37   **Preparing for handover**

K–L/S8   **Post-completion**

K–L/S1   Keeping the client informed

The client will expect to be kept informed about the progress of work and given a regular report on the financial situation. Any material changes in design or construction will need his prior approval.

How this is best handled will depend on the size of the job, the client's own organisation and the stipulated procedures for the project team. A few clients might elect to leave matters almost entirely in the hands of the architect, but the majority will expect formal reports at regular intervals. Some clients will expect to be directly represented at architects' site progress meetings. Matters to be kept in mind include the following:

Time

The client will need to be kept informed about programme and progress. This information will be available through minutes of site progress meetings (issued by the architect), copies of correspondence relating to notices of delay, and the award of any extensions of time.

Quality

The client will need to be kept informed about any problems concerning materials and workmanship, where it becomes necessary to issue architect's instructions. The client should also be advised in good time about such matters as regular maintenance, and the need to appoint or instruct staff about installation requirements, control and maintenance of systems. It might also be necessary for the client to take out maintenance contracts for certain installations.

Cost

The client should receive detailed statements of expenditure at regular intervals, with an appraisal of the current position and a forecast of total costs. The client must agree any extra expenditure in advance, whether this is for unavoidable adjustments in design, or modifications requested by the client, or an adjustment because of provisional sums expenditure. Where possible, it is good policy to have variations costed before the instruction is implemented. Cost reports will normally be prepared by the QS, but where no QS has been appointed (eg on minor works) then these might have to be prepared by the architect. For a typical financial report to client, see Fig KL.01.

Fig KL.01   **Specimen financial report to client**

Job no: Job title:

Financial report to client

To end of (month)	(year)	Savings £	Extras £	£
Financial approvals	Contract sum as adjusted	_____	_____	_____
	Additional approvals to date of last report	_____	_____	_____
	Total approvals to date of last report	_____	_____	_____
Adjustments	Contract sum as adjusted including contingencies	_____	_____	_____
	Cost adjustment on PC sums ordered	_____	_____	_____
	Cost adjustment on provisional sums	_____	_____	_____
	Value of AIs issued to date	_____	_____	_____
	Changes of work anticipated	_____	_____	_____
Contingencies	Original contingencies sum £	_____	_____	_____
	Estimated proportion £ absorbed to date	_____	_____	_____
	Estimated remainder £	_____	_____	_____
Cost of works	Estimated cost of works £ including contingencies sum	_____	_____	_____
Reconciliation	Variations instructed by the employer since last report	_____	_____	_____
	(a) [addition] estimated cost			
	(b) [omission] estimated saving	_____	_____	_____
	Additional approvals to last report	_____	_____	_____
Final estimate	Estimated final expenditure on present information	_____	_____	_____
	Not included in assessments: VAT, fees, other works (eg piling, landscape, advance orders)			

The usual procedure is for the architect to arrange and chair site progress meetings, and for the contractor to arrange and chair production meetings. In addition, the architect will call and chair special meetings including additional design team meetings for as long as the project requires this. There are also site inspections by the architect, which may or may not be formal and which may take place the same day as the site progress meeting.

As a general rule meetings should only be called for a clear purpose, and should only involve those persons necessary for the successful conduct of the business. All meetings should be properly convened with a precise agenda issued in advance and be chaired in a firm and fair manner. All decisions should be clearly minuted.

Architect's site progress meetings

These are essentially policy meetings and should take place at regular intervals (eg the first Tuesday in the month). It is sometimes helpful if they are immediately preceded by site visits. The main business of the meetings will be to receive reports and to agree action necessary as a result. They are not the place to answer routine queries or provide general information. All the people who attend these meetings should have the authority to act.

A standard agenda of items should be maintained, and it is useful to include an 'Action' column. Minutes should be issued by the architect the day after the meeting, to all those named on the agreed distribution list. It is sensible to require that any dissent from the minutes is made in writing with seven days of issue. For a specimen agenda, see Fig KL.02.

Meetings for special purposes

Even with meetings called ad hoc for some special purpose there should still be an agenda and a formal minute of decisions taken. Meetings might be needed for various reasons – for example, with representatives of adjoining owners, or statutory bodies. It might also be necessary to convene further design team meetings during work on site, and as long as they are needed a consistent agenda and format should be maintained. Such business should not be merged with the architect's site progress meetings.

Contractor's production meetings

These are technical meetings with the subcontractors and are arranged by the contractor to take place before the architect's progress meetings. The architect may be asked to attend; if so, he should make a note of any decisions and act appropriately. The contractor should prepare and distribute the minutes.

Site inspections

These are visits by the architect to observe and comment on the contractor's site supervision and examples of his work at intervals appropriate to the stage of construction. This is periodic inspection, which should be carried out to the extent determined by the nature of the work, and as agreed with the client in the appointing document. If more frequent visits or constant inspection are required, then the client should be recommended to appoint a clerk of works or other resident site inspector.

Fig KL.02   **Specimen agenda for architect's site progress meeting**

		ACTION
1	**Minutes of last meeting**	
2	**Contractor's report**	
	– General report	
	– Subcontractors' meeting report	
	– Progress and programme	
	– Health and Safety matters	
	– Causes of delay: claims arising	
	– Information received since last meeting	
	– Information and drawings required	
	– Architect's instructions required	
3	**Clerk of works' report**	
	– Site matters	
	– Quality control monitoring	
	– Lost time	
	— Tests observed and verified	
4	**Consultants' reports**	
	– Structural works	
	– Mechanical works	
	– Electrical works	
5	**Quantity surveyor's report**	
6	**Communications and procedures**	
7	**Contract completion date**	
	– Likely delays and their effect	
	– Review of factors from previous meeting	
	– Factors for review at next meeting	
	– Revision to completion date	
	– Revisions required to programme	
8	**Any other business**	
9	**Date of next meeting**	

The purpose of these visits, whether to the site of the works or to places off site where work is being prepared, is simply to observe and comment. It should not be termed or thought of as 'supervision', because this suggests the authority to issue instructions to operatives, which clearly an architect does not possess.

Visits may be on a periodic basis (eg at fortnightly intervals) or on a predictive basis (eg programmed to match certain stages or operations on site) or as spot checks made without prior warning. It will be for the architect to decide the most appropriate course to adopt, subject to the arrangement with the client.

Visits should have a specific purpose, and they require preparation beforehand. This might mean devising a plan after studying the most recent reports and minutes of meetings. The architect will then visit the site with the purpose of observing particular parts or items and of checking that specified tests are being carried out and verified. Checks of a general nature might include:
- whether quality complies generally with the provisions of the contract;
- whether progress accords with the contractor's master programme;
- whether essential parts of the design have been/are being carried out in accordance with the contract provisions.

Such visits should be carried out carefully, and comments systematically noted. Where certificates refer to work etc 'properly executed', it is helpful to have a record of notes made at the time of a visit. Queries are often raised during site visits, and it may be prudent to reserve answers until returning to the office. Any decisions made or information given while on site should be confirmed in writing as soon as possible.

Reports of site visits should be prepared to a consistent format as soon after the visit as possible. Record photographs (dated), notes and sketches should be attached and carefully filed. These should be retained strictly for in-house use. Fig KL.03 is a specimen site visit report form.

Fig KL.03   **Specimen report form for predictive site visits**

Job no: _____   Job title: _____

Site visit report

Date _____   No. of visits scheduled _____

Visit by _____   Visit no. _____

Purpose
_____
_____
_____
_____
_____
_____
_____
_____
_____

Observed
_____
_____
_____
_____
_____
_____
_____
_____
_____
_____
_____
_____
_____
_____

Checked   **Recorded**

Samples _____   Photos _____

Verification of tests _____   _____

Vouchers _____   Video _____

Records _____   Other _____

Summary   ☐ Work properly executed   ☐ Proceeding in workmanlike manner

                ☐ Materials properly stored and protected   ☐ Progress to programme

Checklist: Setting out

Information
· check that the contractor has setting out information.

Clearance
· check on demolition, site clearance etc.

Fencing, signs
· check security, positions of fencing, hoardings, signs, including architect's design for main signboard etc.

Huts, storage
· check siting of huts, storage, welfare facilities, sanitary fittings etc.

Protective measures
· check that adequate protection is given to property, trees and special features.

Siting of plant
· review contractor's location of major plant against the building structure design, parking and vehicle circulation proposals, and check against Health and Safety Plan.

Spoil heaps
· check siting of spoil deposit areas.

Datum
· check datum and benchmark.

Soil conditions
· examine soil conditions, and treatment of any trial pits, filled basements etc before building.

Setting out, levels
· examine setting out and levels, if necessary.

'As built' information
· check with consultants, clerk of works etc, to record 'as built' information as works proceed (especially underground services). Relevant information should be passed to the Planning Supervisor for inclusion in the Health and Safety File.

General checklist: Site visits

Note
· whether policy on restrictions to visitors to site is being observed;
· whether site facilities continue to be as tendered for;
· whether construction phase Health and Safety Plan is being observed;
· whether fire code is being observed;
· whether contractor's quality plan is being observed;
· contractor's apparent competence, site organisation, labour relations etc.

Check
· workmanship for conformity with drawings and specification;
· workmanship and materials against approved samples where applicable;
· that work is carried out regularly, accurately and in proper sequence;
· that finished work is adequately protected.

Check
· unfixed goods and materials for conformity with specification;
· unfixed goods and materials for storage and protection;
· fixed goods and materials for adequate protection;
· materials against approved samples, where applicable;
· that materials included for in previous certificate have not been removed.

Note
· any requests for information outstanding;
· general progress, any delays and their causes;
· observed noncompliance in workmanship, goods or materials;
· architect's instructions not yet acted upon;
· the results of tests, verification etc required under the contract;
· any site instructions to be confirmed.

Under most building contracts the only person authorised to issue instructions to the contractor will be the contract administrator. It is sensible to establish at the start of the job what constitutes an 'architect's instruction', and it is suggested that only written instructions issued on a standard form should be regarded as valid. The giving of oral instructions, using contractors' site instruction books, or taking the minutes of site meetings as instructions should all be avoided.

The particular form of contract used will state what powers are given to the contract administrator with regard to instructions, and only empowered instructions will bind the contractor. When issuing an instruction it is advisable to check the following:

- that it is empowered under the contract, and the relevant clause number can be cited;
- that the identifying details are entered on the form (eg name of project, contractor, date of instruction, serial number etc);
- that the instructions are precisely worded and their meaning unambiguous;
- that the instruction is signed by the authorised person.

A file copy will be retained, and it is also good practice to keep a record of AIs issued for the project. See Figs KL.04 and KL.05 for specimen forms.

Fig KL.04   Specimen form: Architect's Instruction

Issued by:
address:

Architect's Instruction

Employer:
address:

Job reference:

Instruction no: 4

Contractor:
address:

Issue date:

Sheet: of

Works:
situated at:

Contract dated:

Under the terms of the above-mentioned Contract, I/we issue the following instructions:

	Office use: Approx costs	
	£ omit	£ add
1. HIP TILES OMIT: Farland concrete third round hip tiles, bill of quantities ref.5/15E. ADD in lieu: Red Bank 300mm long red Terracotta third round segmental ridge tiles, list no.259.	372.00	514.00
2. HIP IRONS OMIT: 4 no. hip irons, bill of quantities ref.5/15F. ADD in lieu: 4 no. Red Bank 300mm long red Terracotta Scroll hip finial tiles 225mm diameter. Hip tiles and finial tiles to be obtained from Farbridge Bank Manufacturing Co. Ltd.	---	---

To be signed by or for the issuer named above

Signed _WorBach_

Amount of Contract Sum	£	
± Approximate value of previous Instructions	£	
± Approximate value of this Instruction	£	
Approximate adjusted total	£	

Distribution   Original to: Copies to:

☐ Contractor   ☐ Employer   ☐ Quantity Surveyor   ☐ Clerk of Works

☐ Nominated Sub-Contractors   ☐ Consultants   ☐ File

F809 for JCT 80/IFC 84/MW 80

© RIBA Publications Ltd 1991

Fig KL.05   Specimen record form of architect's instructions issued

Job no: Job title:

Architect's Instructions issued

Date	AI no.		Item	Subject (including relevant item/drawing no.)	Estimated +/- cost (£)
	1		Gas main	Quotation ref 8438/63	+ 150
	2		Cills	Revised detail drwg. L.51/03	− 75
	3		Opening	First floor. revised. drwg. L.51/12	+ 100
	4	(1)	Hip tiles	omit Farsand / add Red Bank	+ 142
		(2)	Hip irons	omit / add finials	

1. Use an AI for all instructions and notifications to the contractor.
2. List all individual items in any AI.
3. Make sure all instructions are clearly worded and unambiguous.
4. Do not reserve numbers for future issue; do not miss out any numbers. If any error in numbering is found, immediately notify everyone on the distribution list.

Although the word is frequently used, 'claim' is something of a misnomer as far as contract administration is concerned. The architect has the authority to act where the contract conditions expressly provide for entitlement in certain events, particularly concerning extensions of time and reimbursement of loss and expense.

Claims not expressly within the contract provisions or where, for various reasons, a contractor has elected not to follow the procedures or is unable to conform to the express terms, would be 'ex-contractual' claims to be pursued in arbitration or litigation.

Extensions of time

Most construction contracts include a mechanism for dealing in a convenient way with events which might affect progress, which are beyond the control of the contractor, and which were not foreseeable at the time of tender. For this to be operable there must be a clearly stated date for possession or commencement, and a date for completion. There is usually an extension of time provision and a separate provision for dealing with additional costs which might arise.

Extensions of time provisions benefit the contractor in that he is relieved of paying liquidated damages for failure to complete because of stated reasons. The express terms are also very much in the client's interests by keeping alive the right to liquidated damages even though the contract period is extended because of his intervention. It is of course essential that such intervention is included as an event covered in the contract conditions, and that the architect operates the extensions of time provisions strictly in accordance with contract requirements.

When dealing with extensions of time, remember the following.
- Respond to each and every proper notice of delay from the contractor – at least it is evidence that his claim has been considered.
- When awarding extensions of time, do so only for the causes specified in the contract. State the causes, but do not apportion. Keep full records in case the award is contested.
- Comply strictly with the procedural rules. For example, if the contract requires it, notify every nominated subcontractor of a decision.
- Observe the timescale if one is stated in the contract. If none is stated, act within a reasonable time.
- Form an opinion which is fair and reasonable in the light of the information available at the time.

Loss and/or expense applications

Monetary claims arising in the context of building contracts are usually made as a result of loss due to regular progress being affected or because of additional costs due to a prolongation of the time on site. The wording in the contract usually identifies events or matters which are recognised as causes. There may be procedures to be followed which exist for the convenience of both parties. It is only these types of claims which the architect administering the contract has the authority to settle.

For an application to be valid:
· the loss and/or expense must be a *direct* actual loss;
· the works (or a part) must be materially affected;
· interference or disturbance to regular planned progress must have occurred;
· reimbursement must not be possible under any other contractual provision.

The architect has a duty to decide whether the claim is valid and, if information supplied is not adequate, additional reasonably necessary information must be requested.

Ascertainment of the amount claimed can rest with the architect, but normally the contract allows specifically for this function to be referred to the QS.

When dealing with applications for reimbursement, remember the following.
· The object of these provisions is to put the contractor back into the position he would have been but for the disruption. It is not an opportunity to profit.
· The contractor must make written application at the proper time.
· The architect must form an opinion about whether direct loss and/or expense has been incurred or is likely to be incurred, and that regular progress has been materially affected.
· The burden of proof rests with the contractor. If the notice is not sufficient, more information must be requested.
· Ascertainment is a matter of certainty and not approximation. Particularisation of claims, ie 'actual' figures relating to specific items, should be expected.

The importance of keeping good records cannot be emphasised too strongly. It is recommended that a record should be kept of site delays observed or noted from reports; defective work observed which might relate to subsequent applications when instructions are issued; a schedule of 'claims' submitted by the contractor which need to be noted and acted upon. For specimen record forms, see Figs KL.06, KL.07 and KL.08. Fig KL.09 is a specimen letter in reply to a contractor 'claiming' loss and expense without following the contract procedures.

Fig KL.06   Specimen record form of site delays observed

Job no: Job title:

Record of site delays observed

Date	Delay	Item	Reason	Observed by
6.1.95	1 week	Site clearance	Plant hire equipment late	C of W
17.1.95	1 week	Weather	Heavy snow	C of W
23.2.95	3 days	Foundations	Excavations waterlogged	C of W
10.4.95	2 days	Steelwork	Erectors arrived. Problem with crane jib. Left site.	HRJ

1. Record observations in sequence of work element/location, conditions or situation and note the source of information where relevant.
2. Liaise closely with clerk of works and consultants.
3. Check against and coordinate with your site inspection reports.

Fig KL.07   **Specimen record form of defective work**

Job no:	Job title:			

Record of defective work

Date	Item	Contractor notified	Value if deducted	Cleared
		Date	£	Date
1.8.95	Priming to some steelwork unsatisfactory	2.8.95		2.9.95
16.9.95	Nosing to boiler house steps not satisfactory. Shuttering poor	16.9.95		12.10.95

1. Describe the work in sequence of work element/location: condition as rejected: rectification required.
2. Check and update this record regularly with clerk of works and consultants.
3. Notify QS of any values deducted against valuations made and when items are cleared.
4. Check against and coordinate with your site inspection reports.

Fig KL.08   Specimen record form of claims by contractor

Job no: Job title:

Schedule of claims by contractor

Date received	Clause no.	Subject of claim	Time/amount: Req'std	Allowed	Date for decision	Date awarded
25.2.95	25	Weather – notice of delay inadequate – more detailed information requested				
		AI No. 1				
	25	Gas main	4 days	2 days		
	26	Consequential loss/expense				

1. Check that contractor uses procedures laid down in the contract.
2. Inform QS, consultants, clerk of works immediately any claim is notified.
3. List adequate description and if necessary open a sub-file to collate the correspondence etc about each claim.
4. Check that your action complies with the time limits stated in the contract.

Fig KL.09   **Specimen letter in reply to a contractor's unsubstantiated claim**

Thank you for your notification that the regular progress of the
work has been materially affected and that this may give rise to
an application for the reimbursement of direct loss and expense
under Clause 26 of JCT 80.

Would you please state which of the list of matters you consider
apply in this instance, and forward such information that you
consider will reasonably enable us to form an opinion, including
your reasons as to why you cannot recover the cost under any
other condition.

Should we be of the opinion that the delay is covered by Clause
26, you will of course be required to provide [the quantity
surveyor with] such details as are reasonably necessary to
ascertain the direct loss and/or expense.

Contracts generally provide for the issue of certificates by the contract administrator. The issue will normally be an obligation, always subject to certain conditions being satisfied. A certificate is simply a statement of fact, and although a letter might constitute a certificate, it is advisable to establish at the beginning of the job that valid certificates will be those issued on a standard form.

Certificates commonly provided for in a contract may include the following:

Interim certificate
(see Fig KL.10)

This is for payment to the contractor – an instalment on account. It might be on a monthly valuation (although the architect when certifying must use skill and care, and not blindly follow the QS's valuation), on a stage or milestone basis as agreed by the parties and in accordance with the contract conditions.

Certificate of non-completion

A factual statement, upon which much may depend, eg the deduction of liquidated damages by the employer, or the right to deduct damages by a main contractor against a nominated subcontractor etc.

Certificate of practical completion
(see Fig KL.11)

A statement which expresses that for all practical purposes the contractor has discharged his contractual duties and is relieved from various obligations henceforth.

Certificate of making good defects

Issued only when those defects listed at the close of the defects liability period have been remedied.

Final certificate
(see Fig KL.13)

Issue of the final certificate brings the authority of the contract administrator, under the terms of the building contract, to a close. The contractor's liability continues of course until the end of the limitation period.

There might, in addition or alternatively, be contract provisions which refer to Statements issued by the contract administrator or by the Employer (eg in the case of design and build contracts). These should be regarded as requiring the same care and consideration before issue as certificates. Recent case law has confirmed that there is no immunity from negligence in certifying.

Fig KL.10   **Specimen form: Interim Certificate and Direction**

**Interim
Certificate
and Direction**

Issued by:
address:

Employer: Serial no: **D**
address:

                                                                 Job reference:

Contractor: Certificate no:
address:

                                                                 Issue date:

Works: Valuation date:
situated at:

                                                                 Contract sum:

Contract dated: 6 December 1993, read with the Declaration dated | Original to Employer |
                 2 March 1995

This Interim Certificate is issued under the terms of the above-mentioned
Contract.

Gross valuation inclusive of the value of works by Nominated
Sub-Contractors .... £   247,260.00

Less Retention which may be retained by the Employer as detailed on
the Statement of Retention .... £   12,417.00

                                              Sub-total £   235,843.00

Less total amount stated as due in Interim Certificates previously
issued up to and including Interim Certificate no: 7 .... £   208,133.00

Net amount for payment .... £   27,710.00

I/We hereby certify that the **amount for payment** by the Employer to the
Contractor on this Certificate is (in words)
Twenty-seven thousand seven hundred and ten pounds

I/We hereby direct the Contractor that this amount includes interim or
final payments to Nominated Sub-Contractors as listed in the attached
Statement of Retention and of Nominated Sub-Contractors' Values, which
are to be discharged to those named in accordance with the Sub-Contract.

Note: The issue of this
certificate is not for and shall
not be taken as showing that
any work or materials or
goods or workmanship is or
are accepted as conforming to
description or being in
accordance with The Contract.

All amounts are exclusive of VAT

To be signed by or for
the issuer named
above   Signed _Worbach_

[1] Relevant only if   [1] The Contractor has given notice that the rate of VAT chargeable on the
clause 1A of the VAT   supply of goods and services to which the Contract relates is 17.5 %
Agreement applies.
Delete if not
applicable.   [1] 17.5 % of the amount certified above is .... £   4,848.00

                       [1] Total of net amount and VAT amount (for information) .... £   32,558.00

This is not a Tax Invoice

F801 for JCT 80   ©RIBA Publications Ltd 1990

Fig KL.11   **Specimen form: Certificate of Practical Completion**

Certificate of

Practical Completion

Issued by:
address:

Employer:
address:

Job reference:

Certificate no:

Contractor:
address:

Issue date:

Works:
situated at:

Contract dated: 6 December 1993, read with the Declaration dated
2 March 1995

Under the terms of the above-mentioned Contract,

I/we hereby certify that Practical Completion of

*Delete as
appropriate

*1. the Works

~~*2. Section No.~~ _____ ~~of the Works~~

was achieved on

1 March   **19** 95

Note: The issue of this
certificate is not for and shall
not be taken as showing that
any work or materials or
goods or workmanship is or
are accepted as conforming to
description or being in
accordance with The Contract.

To be signed by or for
the issuer named
above

Signed _wor Batch_____

Distribution	Original to:	Duplicate to:	Copies to:	
	☐ Employer	☐ Contractor	☐ Quantity Surveyor	☐ Clerk of Works
			☐ Consultants	☐ File

F853 for JCT 80/IFC 84/MW 80   © RIBA Publications Ltd 1991

Fig KL.12   Specimen record form of defects reported after practical completion

Job no: Job title:

Defects reported after practical completion

Date reported	Location of defect	Description	Health and Safety implications

Fig KL.13   **Specimen form: Final Certificate**

Issued by:
address:

Employer:
address:

Contractor:
address:

Works:
situated at:

Contract dated: 6 December 1993, read with the Declaration dated
2 March 1995 stating as shown below ★

**Final
Certificate**

A

Serial no: **A**

Job reference:

Issue date:

Contract sum:

| Original to Employer |

This Final Certificate is issued under the terms of the above-mentioned
Contract.

The Contract Sum adjusted as necessary is . . . .   £   311,187.00

The total amount previously certified for payment to the Contractor is . . . .   £   302,064.00

The difference between the above-stated amounts is . . . .   £   9,123.00

I/We hereby certify the sum of (in words)
Nine thousand one hundred and twenty three pounds only

as a **balance due**:

*Delete as
appropriate

*to the Contractor from the Employer.

*to the Employer from the Contractor.

All amounts are exclusive of VAT

To be signed by or for
the issuer named
above

Signed _____

★ "For the avoidance or removal of doubt it is
mutually declared, acknowledged and agreed that
the final certificate or any other certificate issued
by the Architect
is not intended to and shall not operate as
conclusive evidence that any of the work or
materials or goods or workmanship conforms to
description or is in accordance with The Contract."

The terms of the Contract provide that, subject to any amounts properly
deductible by the Employer, the said balance shall be a debt payable from
the one to the other as from the

[1] Delete as
appropriate. See cover
notes for provision in
particular contract.

[1] 14th / 21st / 28th day after the date of this Certificate.

Note: The issue of this
certificate is not for and shall
not be taken as showing that
any work or materials or
goods or workmanship is or
are accepted as conforming to
description or being in
accordance with The Contract.

[2] Relevant only if
clause 1A of JCT 80
VAT Agreement,
clause A1·1 of IFC 84
Supplemental
Conditions or clause
B1·1 of MW 80
Supplementary
Memorandum applies.
Delete if not
applicable.

[2] The Contractor has given notice that the rate of VAT chargeable on the
supply of goods and services to which the Contract relates is   17.5   %

[2] 17.5   % of the amount certified above is . . . .   £   1,594.00

[2] Total of balance due and VAT amount (for information) . . . .   £   10,717.00

This is not a Tax Invoice

F852 for JCT 80 / IFC 84 / MW 80

© RIBA Publications Ltd 1990

Although not usually referred to in building contracts, the process of completion and handing over the building should nevertheless be subject to careful planning and procedures. It is suggested that these should comprise:

- final commissioning, testing and witnessing of services installations;
- pre-completion checks by the contract administrator;
- preparation for the formal handing over;
- issue of the practical completion certificate;
- the formal handover meeting.

Normally the contract administrator can expect to be advised by the contractor when the works are approaching practical completion. Sometimes this indication is premature. Sometimes the client will pressure the contract administrator to certify prematurely. The contract administrator should act strictly in accordance with the conditions of the contract. The parties are free to agree an expedient arrangement outside the contract terms if they so wish. The following is based on guidance published in RIBA *Practice*, issue 82, February 1992.

Possession by Client or Employer before practical completion

It is not uncommon for the Employer, after the completion date has passed, to wish to take possession of the works before the Contractor has achieved practical completion. In this event an ad hoc agreement between Employer and Contractor is required to deal with the situation, and RIBA members may wish to note the following.

Where it is known to the architect that there are outstanding items, practical completion should not be certified without specially agreed arrangements between the Employer and the Contractor. For example, in the case of a contract where the contract completion date has passed, it could be so agreed that the incomplete building will be taken over for occupation, subject to postponing the release of retention and the beginning of the defects liability period until the outstanding items referred to in a list to be prepared by the architect have been completed, but relieving the Contractor from liability for liquidated damages for delay as from the date of occupation, and making any necessary changes in the insurance arrangements.

In such circumstances either the certificate of practical completion form should not be used, or it should be altered to state or refer to the specially agreed arrangements. In making such arrangements the architect should have the authority of the Client-Employer.

Final commissioning, testing and witnessing of services installation

Commissioning is the process whereby static completion of an installation is brought to the state of full working order for proving. Testing is a matter of checking a commissioned installation and evaluating its performance measured against specified requirements. Commissioning and testing are operations which, on a sophisticated project, might need to be carried out by specialists, will need to be effectively managed, and should be subject to a commissioning specification and system for commissioning. They might also need to be phased, and although the installations will need to be commissioned before handover, some adjustment and testing might not be possible until after installations have been in use for a certain period.

Almost every project includes a services installation, and proper thought is needed at the outset concerning design, installation, inspection and arrangements for commissioning and testing. Many larger client bodies expect particular codes to be observed and stated procedures to be followed. The Chartered Institution of Building Services Engineers publishes a series of Commissioning Codes which clearly itemise the checks necessary for various installations. The Building Services Research and Information Association publishes a guide to operating and maintenance manuals for building services installations. Reference to appropriate documents such as these will normally be made when specifying methods of commissioning.

Tender documents should clearly state the level of commissioning and testing which will be required, both before handover and additionally perhaps with a defects liability period of appropriate duration. Thought should also be given to the need for incorporating special conditions of contract, because most standard forms do not make specific reference to such matters.

Where services installations are of a complex nature, it is likely that consultants and specialist firms will be involved, and expert commissioning engineers might need to be brought in. Nevertheless, the main contractor still has the responsibility for overall programming, and for ensuring that the works are finished by the contract completion date. This will usually necessitate commissioning, testing, and the preparation of operating or maintenance manuals before handover. Sometimes difficulties arise where these latter operations are not allocated sufficient time, or where the costs entailed have not been fully covered in the contract sum.

A common difficulty is the precise definition of responsibilities. Architects will obviously have a responsibility to see that requirements are properly included for and stated at the outset. Manufacturers will also have a responsibility, particularly where use of particular components is specified. Inspection of services installations as work proceeds may be largely in the hands of consultants and subcontractors, although the main contractor will ultimately remain responsible for all matters of workmanship and materials. Whilst architects will have a duty to see what appropriate arrangements are made for commissioning and testing, responsibility for carrying out such operations should clearly lie with others.

The following checklist is based on guidance published in RIBA *Practice*, issue 78, September 1991.

Checklist for commissioning

During contract

Installing might involve:
· inspecting during construction – making preliminary checks, visual checks, electrical checks, mechanical checks, pneumatic checks etc, which will include cleanliness, frost protection and leak testing;
· testing of individual components – pipework, ductwork etc as work proceeds, whether with electrical supplies isolated or available if appropriate;
· ensuring permanent electrical, gas, water etc and fuel connections;
· making all connections to main control panels and checking distribution.

Commissioning might involve:
· Setting to work all static systems into motion (eg fans, heaters, pumps, starting up boilers etc after checking pressurisation equipment, tanks and pipe runs). Making initial settings of valves , dampers and other actuators;
· regulating and adjusting the systems to the specified tolerances; checking out, calibrating and setting up etc;
· testing control and alarm systems; emergency and fire circuits, safety controllers and electrical overload equipment;
· balancing water supply systems, flow check rates, radiators, regulating air flow and extract air dampers, checking tolerances.

Testing before completion might involve:
· Recording test results and final settings of all dampers, thermostats, overload settings; checking temperatures, access, failsafe devices; evaluating and witnessing systems;
· completing schematic and other 'as fitted' drawings and manuals of operating instructions;
· demonstrating operation of equipment and making employer's maintenance operatives familiar with procedures; producing evidence of continuous unattended running records;
· topping up fuel, renewing filters, tubes and other components etc as necessary;
· handing over at practical completion.

Post-completion

Performance testing might involve carrying out performance tests to prove the performance of the commissioned equipment over a full climatic cycle at appropriate times prior to the expiry of the defects liability period. The climatic cycle should be specified – usually 12 months or at least extending to a full heating season.

It is suggested that commissioning and testing procedures should be programmed for all but the smallest contracts. Architects who are acting without the assistance of specialist consultants might find it very useful to produce their own bar charts to ensure that M & E services are properly commissioned before handover.

On larger projects with more complex installations, a great deal can be done to make sure that responsibilities are clearly established and that the main contractor is ultimately responsible for much of the testing and verification, albeit with specialist assistance.

There should generally be only one defects liability period for both building and installations. If the testing cycle needs to extend beyond the defects liability period, this should be clearly stated and provided for under the contract.

Pre-completion checks by the contract administrator

Pre-completion checks

· Warn contractor to make sure that the building is ready for inspection well before the date of practical completion;
· instruct clerk of works to maintain systematic preliminary inspections and to keep the architect informed of progress and any difficulties likely to arise as well as defects discovered;
· consolidate a schedule of outstanding items from:
  – architect's progress meeting minutes
  – consultants' reports
  – clerk of works' reports
  – architect's instructions
  – site visit notes.
· Instruct contractor to carry out any remedial works required;
· remind contractor to complete record drawings etc according to the agreed programme.

Inspection and commissioning

· In collaboration with consultants, advise contractor and all subcontractors to coordinate a programme of checks;
· instruct clerk of works accordingly and ensure he checks that defective work has been replaced and reports any delays anticipated, where relevant asking client's staff to attend inspections and checks;
· ask consultants to make detailed inspections and report back;
· check that associated contractors' works are completed;
· issue instructions to contractor for subcontractors to carry out outstanding and/or remedial works following the inspections;
· remind subcontractors to complete record drawings etc and to prepare maintenance instructions as agreed;
· make formal arrangements with client for handover inspections.

Preparation for the formal handover

Before the meeting

· Remind the client of the reasonable standards which are appropriate to the class of work specified. It is the architect's responsibility to certify;
· inform the client's representative of the basis of the contract (if he has not been personally involved from the start);
· write to the contractor and all those who are to attend the meeting to let them know the time, date and venue.

Inspecting the buildings and site

· Hold meeting(s) for inspection and handover;
· check that the following are ready to hand over as required:
  – building owner's operating manual
  – keys
  – as built drawings
  – details of maintenance arrangements
  – Health and Safety File.
· Outline the client's and contractor's responsibilities during the defects liability period;
· outline arrangements for dealing with any future defects;
· agree any additional works required by the client.

Defects

· Confirm in writing within 14 days any defects and remedial works to be carried out, marking items which are urgent. Copy to contractor, clerk of works, consultants and client;
· periodically check progress and work executed.

Additional works
- Liaise with the QS and contractor to negotiate the basis for pricing;
- prepare drawings and instructions and obtain the client's approval of these and the related costs;
- instruct the contractor to proceed (by means of an extension of the contract, or a separate agreed instruction);
- check that these are covered by the construction phase Health and Safety Plan.

Issue of the practical completion certificate

There may be a number of 'completion certificates' which the contract administrator is obliged to issue. For example:
- Statement of partial possession (where practical completion is deemed to have occurred).
- Practical completion for sectional completion.
- Practical completion for nominated subcontract works.
- Practical completion of 'the Works'.

It is the latter which triggers off a sequence of events, namely:
- The contractor's liability for damage to the completed works is ended.
- The contractor's liability for any further liquidated damages is ended.
- The contractor's liability for insurance of the works is ended.
- The contractor's liability for damage to the works as a result of frost is ended.
- Half the retention money is usually released to the contractor.
- Reference to arbitration on matters previously barred by the contract conditions may be opened.

The practical completion certificate (see Fig KL.11) is issued only when in the opinion of the contract administrator (or other person referred to expressly in the contract) the works have reached a state of practical completion.

The formal handover meeting

The arrangements listed will be relevant in nearly all cases, including where there is sectional completion or partial possession.

Record attendance, date etc

Define purpose of meeting
- Explain that inspections of building and site are to establish agreement that work is ready to hand over to the client for occupation;
- note defects due to faulty workmanship or materials and issue instructions to the contractor to rectify them, immediately if appropriate;
- ensure that all contractor's plant and property have been removed from site.

Tour of inspection
- Inspect building(s) and site.

Handover of building
Client accepts building and site from contractor, and
contractor hands over keys.
- Ensure that meters have been read and fuel stocks noted.

Maintenance manuals, servicing contracts etc.
Confirm with Planning Supervisor contents of Health and Safety File, and arrangements for delivering it to the client.

· Hand over any further building maintenance information as relevant, including:
- directory
- servicing contracts
- maintenance of plant
- maintenance of building
- attention to landscape and planting
- routine replacement schedules
- record or as built drawings as applicable.

Fig KL.14 is an outline contents for a client's handbook or maintenance manual.

Fig KL.14   **Contents for a client's maintenance handbook**

The following is a list of matters which should normally be included in a handbook. The degree of detail will be determined by the nature of the project and the purpose for which the handbook is intended. In many cases it will form part of the Health and Safety File.

1 Sources of information

This will be a directory and compilation of schedules. It might include:
- a description of the building suitable for publicity material, including design objectives and philosophy;
- photographs taken during construction and on completion (dated and referenced);
- names and addresses of consultants and their respective contributions;
- contract information, including key dates;
- a list of statutory authorities concerned, with copies of consents or approvals obtained;
- a list of subcontractors and suppliers, with names of contacts;
- details of emergency contacts;
- a list and details of the location of materials which might be considered injurious or hazardous under certain circumstances;
- details of structural composition or assembly, about which warnings should be given when dismantling or demolition is being considered;
- a schedule of floor areas and designed permissible loadings;
- a list of special maintenance contracts which should be considered (eg lift installations, fire alarms or sprinkler installations).

2 General maintenance guidance

General maintenance might include a clear introductory statement on the obvious but often overlooked importance of regular maintenance. In common with all man-made objects, buildings start to deteriorate from the time of completion, and regular programmed maintenance is essential. Other items included might be:
- instructions for regular cleaning;
- a general maintenance guide chart;
- general maintenance instructions (which should include reference to safe systems for maintenance work incorporated into the design);
- general maintenance log sheets for completion by maintenance staff or in-house or contracted engineers.
- details and description of fittings which might need regular replacement.

3 Services and specialist maintenance

This might include:
- a services maintenance guide chart, including timing and frequency;
- details of fittings for routine replacement;
- maintenance log sheets for completion by staff;
- a list of drawings which accompany the manual.

Defects liability

Once practical completion is reached, the defects liability period starts to run. Under this convenient contractual arrangement the employer may give the contractor an opportunity to rectify certain defects which have arisen, at the contractor's own cost. Defects will not include damage inflicted during this period, nor should defects liability be confused with maintenance.

On practical completion the architect should:
- fix the date for the defects liability inspection;
- advise the employer to list any defects as they become apparent, and notify immediately those defects which should receive attention during the defects liability period;
- prepare a draft schedule of defects (see Fig KL.12) as a checklist for the defects liability inspection;
- carry out an inspection at the end of the defects liability period accompanied by the employer, contractor, and clerk of works if available;
- complete a schedule of defects and deliver it to the contractor within 14 days of the expiry of the defects liability period;
- arrange for a programme of remedial work, with the agreement of the employer and contractor;
- determine whether remedial work is subject to compliance with CDM Regulations and advise contractor accordingly;
- carry out a final inspection after defects have been remedied;
- issue a certificate that defects have been made good when satisfied.

The final account

Final adjustments to the contract sum should be made in accordance with the conditions of the contract, and to the timescale and procedures stated. Deductions and additions as necessary will result in the sum for the final account. Where the sum is agreed with the contractor, then subject to any provisos expressed in the contract, preparations can be made to issue the final certificate. Where the sum is not agreed by the contractor, then if the architect and QS are in agreement over the figure, it may be necessary to inform the employer and proceed with the issue of the final certificate nonetheless.

The architect should:
- review the progress of the final account each month with the QS, checking on outstanding items;
- estimate the date for completing the final account after consulting the QS and consultants;
- obtain from the QS a statement of outstanding claims from the contractor and subcontractors and their financial implications, if necessary calling a meeting with the QS and contractor to resolve them;
- resolve specialists' outstanding claims at a meeting with consultants if necessary;
- keep the client informed of the progress of the final account and any significant cost adjustments arising from claims;
- report the value of the final account to the client when the QS sends it to the contractor for final agreement;
- when it is agreed, start procedures for issuing the final certificate;
- if necessary, and only if authorised by the client, arrange for separate accounts for works ordered after practical completion.

The final certificate

The final certificate (see Fig KL.13) effectively terminates the opportunity for any further discussion and brings the authority and power of the contract administrator under the contract to an end.

Either party will be able to challenge the certificate to the extent and subject to the timescale expressed in the contract conditions.

The contractor's obligations under the contract are at an end, although he will still be liable for the duration of the limitation period applicable.

The architect should:
- check that the final inspection with consultants has been carried out, that all defects have been made good to the architect's satisfaction, and that a certificate of making good has been issued;
- arrange for the release of the remainder of the retention monies where relevant;
- write to the contractor to return drawings and other documents, where relevant;
- receive the final account and final valuation from the QS, referring it to the local authority or other official or auditor as required;
- issue the final certificate in accordance with the contract conditions;
- agree with the client which documents he wishes to retain.

Feedback

M

M/1   **Activities**

M/2   **Actions**

M/3   **Stage summary**

M/4   **Watchpoints**

M/5   **Action checks**

Supplement

M/S1   Keeping office records

M/S2   In-house appraisal

M/S3   Debriefing

M/S4   Full feedback study

Description

Stage M Feedback was shown in the RIBA's *Plan of Work* as printed in the 1967 issue of the *Handbook of Architectural Practice and Management*. It was not listed in *Architect's Appointment*, nor is it referred to in current standard appointing documents.

On completion of a project there will always be need to assemble documents for retention, and to compile records. This is an activity appropriate to nearly all projects. A study of such material could lead to an updating of the office systems to take account of lessons learned. There are then three levels at which further post-completion studies may be carried out.

First, there can be an investigation or appraisal restricted to an in-house operation. Second, there may be a debriefing exercise which could involve other people concerned with the project, and this could commence shortly after completion. Third, there could be a full feedback study, and this is unlikely to be possible until several years after completion.

Debriefing is a term not referred to in *Plan of Work*, but it can provide useful lessons for the client and members of both the design and the construction teams. It will require the setting up of a series of meetings which need to be carefully structured and conducted. It is a sensitive area, and confrontation should be avoided at all costs. It will not therefore be a productive exercise in all cases and great care needs to be taken in deciding whether or not it will be worthwhile for a particular project. Both in-house appraisals and debriefing are exercises not normally listed in the services provided by the architect and are unlikely to be funded by the client.

The purpose of a full feedback study is to analyse the management, construction and performance of a project. This could entail:
- an analysis of the project records;
- an inspection of the fabric of the completed building;
- studies of the building in use.

A full feedback study can be costly, and if the client wishes this to be undertaken, it will probably have to be the subject of a separate commission.

Terminology

* The RIBA Outline Plan of Work refers to Stage M Feedback.

* RIBA standard appointing documents do not refer to Stage M.

General procedures

- Preparation of 'as built' drawings and maintenance manuals are included already under Stage K–L.

- Debriefing and feedback are management exercises. If it is agreed to extend the commission to include for these, establish the scope and content of Stage M.

- Agree with the client the extent of professional services to be provided. Agree with the client the methods and levels of charging.

- Effective debriefing might constitute a series of meetings involving architect and client, design team, and architect and contractor.

- Agree with the client body whom from its organisation should be consulted, and with what objectives in mind.

- If a full feedback study is planned, agree with the client what access will be available, what the timescale should be, and in what form the findings should be presented.

Preliminary issues

Concerning the client

- Explain to the client the purpose of a project appraisal and how debriefing or feedback might be an essential part of this activity.

- Discuss with the client to what extent key persons in the organisation could be expected to contribute opinions at a meeting chaired by the architect.

- Discuss with the client to what extent the managers and users of the project could be expected to cooperate in completing a questionnaire.

- Discuss with the client whether authorised photographers would be allowed access after final completion, for feedback purposes.

- Discuss with the client whether it would be permissible for the architect to carry out a survey of the building in use some time after completion.

Team working

- Raise with all consultants the desirability of engaging in a systematic analysis of the management, construction and performance of the project.

- Convene debriefing meetings upon completion to evaluate technical matters, to involve all design team members, the main contractor and possibly the client.

Stage output

Tangible results/material produced before the conclusion of Stage M might include the following as relevant:

· Record of conclusions reached at debriefing meetings, distributed only to participants.

· Results of any surveys conducted with client or user client, or everyday users of the building, perhaps several years post-completion.

* Post-completion studies require a regular and continuous process of assembling important information and records relating to the history of the project.

* In-house appraisal is a healthy operation for nearly all projects, but participants must feel able to exchange views freely.

* It is essential that the benefits and lessons learned from appraisals are passed to all members of staff. The office quality plan, manuals and procedures might need amendment or revision as a result.

* Debriefing can become a sensitive matter and will only succeed with the full cooperation of all involved.

* At debriefing meetings, watch out for partisan or defensive attitudes. Honest and objective discussion should not be allowed to degenerate into acrimony.

* Do not allow an exercise to be undertaken if it seems likely that it might result in recriminations – and even arbitration or litigation.

		Tick if relevant	Initial if completed
01	Collate all documents issued to contractor and store		
02	Collate 'state of the art' trade information etc and store		
03	Conduct in-house appraisal of office performance on project		
04	Revise/update office quality plan, manual, procedures		
05	Consider desirability of a debriefing exercise		
06	Check if client would cooperate in debriefing		
07	Check if design and production teams would cooperate in debriefing		
08	Assess resources needed for debriefing		
09	Arrange series of debriefing meetings		
10	Record discussions and issue report with conclusions		
11	Formulate overall conclusions from debriefing		
12	Circulate findings of debriefing as appropriate		
13	Consider desirability of a full feedback study		
14	Consult client over access and cooperation with interviewers		
15	Arrange programme of feedback interviews		
16	Carry out interviews and visits		
17	Conduct evaluation of finishes, materials etc, in-use studies		
18	Produce report on feedback study		
19	Circulate findings of feedback study as appropriate		
20			
21			
22			
23			
24			
25			
26			
27			
28			
29			
30			

Supplement

M

M/S1   **Keeping office records**

M/S2   **In-house appraisal**

M/S3   **Debriefing**

M/S4   **Full feedback study**

Once a job is complete, a decision has to be made about which drawings and documents should be kept. No office has the space to keep all project records indefinitely.

A set of project records, properly maintained and completed, should be a useful condensed history of the project – a point of reference for quick comparison of working methods, timescales and costs. Photographs of the work in progress and as completed, presentation drawings and models should also be kept available for showing to prospective clients and for publicity purposes generally. However, it is essential to keep proper records of the kind of information that will be required in the event of disputes, in particular:

- the client brief and related correspondence;
- the contract documents;
- architects instructions;
- minutes of project meetings;
- certificates issued;
- notes of inspections, surveys;
- any crucial state-of-the-art information (manufacturers' key information, current BSs, Codes etc);
- progress charts etc;
- selected working drawings.

It is important to remember that the personnel involved with the project may not be available to give evidence if litigation occurs some years later.

Appraise the project under the headings given in the following checklist:

1 Office costs
Relate office costs to reserve and profit targets.

2 Performance of design team, site inspectorate in terms of:
- communications with client
- communications between design team members
- communications with Planning Supervisor
- communications with contractor
- design team programming
- quality of drawings, specifications
- cost planning, final costs against budget
- quality control
- energy effectiveness
- meeting completion date(s) etc.

3 Contractor's performance in terms of:
- project management, quality of staff
- site management, quality of staff
- health and safety compliance
- continuity of personnel
- quality of work
- effectiveness of programming
- cooperation in settling claims
- cooperation over material for Health and Safety File

4 Working arrangements between design team and contractor in terms of:
- architect's progress meetings, actions on minutes
- quality control
- early identification of problems relating to progress, information, quality
- potential disputes
- financial arrangements, certificates, dayworks, measurement evaluation.

5 Completed works in terms of:
- resolution of the brief
- relation to site and surroundings
- quality of building, functional and abstract
- incorporation of M & E services into structure
- energy efficiency
- wear and tear, maintenance.

6 Prepare reports
Include proposals for long term reviews; distribute, file as appropriate.

7 Complete project records:
- collect all relevant project records and information
- collate material and keep available for quick reference and comparison with that of other completed jobs
- arrange photographs for record and/or promotional purposes.

Obtaining valuable lessons with the benefit of hindsight is unlikely to be an activity commissioned by most clients. For a few this might be a worthwhile exercise, and for a truly objective report, impartial 'auditors' could be engaged.

Debriefing after completion is something which should happen in all major projects to some extent. A series of meetings convened by the architect who acted as lead consultant could achieve this, as follows:

- meetings between architect and client to evaluate the management of the project generally;
- meetings between architect and Planning Supervisor to evaluate matters related to compliance with the CDM Regulations;
- meetings between key design team members and contractor to evaluate design and technical aspects of the project;
- meetings between architect and contractor to evaluate the management of the construction of the project.

A frank exchange of views might be expected at meetings, and the success of the operation will depend very much on the cooperation of all parties involved. Opinions on, for example, the overall timescale, the effectiveness of cost control, whether AIs including variations could have been avoided, whether drawings production and issue could have been improved, whether site reporting and quality control were effective etc, might provide valuable lessons for future projects. Obviously the time spent on this kind of operation and the cost of meetings has to be weighed against the fact that the project is usually a 'once only' occurrence, and the particular team might never again be assembled.

The more intensive investigations for feedback, which might not be practicable until several years after completion of the project, could include structured interviews with the client's staff or with users, access to the buildings, access to information and records held by various team members.

Neither of these kinds of activities should be attempted if there is a risk of inviting acrimony and dispute.

References and further reading

A list of supporting material and information which busy practitioners and/or Part 3 candidates might need to have readily available.

Practice	**Professional Liability** Cecil R. 3rd edition 1991	**The Architect's Guide to Running a Job** Green R. 5th edition 1995
	The Architect in Practice Chappell D. and Willis C. 7th edition 1995	**Plan of Work for Design Team Operation** (RIBA 1973)

Legal	**Collateral Warranties Explained** Paterson F.A. (RIBA Publications 1991)	**Loss and Expense Explained** Newman P. & Whitfield G. (RIBA Publications 1994)
	Copyright Explained Delemore C.L. (RIBA Publications 1994)	**Professional Indemnity Insurance Explained** Paterson F.A. (RIBA Publications 1995)
	Extensions of Time Explained Birkby G. & Brough P. (RIBA Publications 1993)	**The 1990–91 Planning Acts** Hope D. (RIBA Publications 1992)
	Insolvency Explained Newman P. (RIBA Publications 1992)	

Appointing Documents	**RIBA Standard Form of Agreement for the Appointment of an Architect (SFA/92)** · Historic Buildings: Alternative Schedule of Services · Community Architecture: Supplementary Schedule of Services · Supplement to take account of CDM Regulations 1994	**SFA Design and Build Guide** A Guide to the Standard Form of Agreement for the Appointment of an Architect for Design and Build (RIBA Publications 1992)
	RIBA Standard Form of Agreement for the Appointment of an Architect, Design and Build · Employer Client version · Contractor Client version	**RIBA Conditions of Engagement for the Appointment of an Architect** (CE/95) **RIBA Form of Appointment as Planning Supervisor** (PS/95)
	SFA Guide A Guide to the Standard Form of Agreement for the Appointment of an Architect (SFA/92) (RIBA Publications 1992)	

Quality Management	**British Standard BS 5750/ISO 9001**, in particular Quality Systems and Guidelines for Quality Plans	**Quality Management – Guidance for an Office Manual** (RIBA 1990)
	British Standard BS 7000/ISO 9001, in particular Guide to Managing Design in the Construction Industry	

References and further reading

Health and Safety

The Workplace (Health, Safety and Welfare) Regulations 1992 (SI 1992 No. 3004)

The Construction (Design and Management) Regulations 1994 (SI 1994 No. 3140)

Managing Construction for Health and Safety – Approved Code of Practice (HSE Books 1995)

Designing for Health and Safety in Construction – A Guide for Designers on the Construction (Design and Management Regulations) 1994 (HSE Books 1995)

Engaging an Architect: Guidance for Clients on Health and Safety – The CDM Regulations (RIBA 1995)

Tendering

NJCC Codes of Procedure
· for Single Stage Selective Tendering
· for Two Stage Selective Tendering
· for Selective Tendering for Design and Build
· for the Letting and Management of Domestic Subcontract Works
· for the Selection of a Management Contractor and Works Contractors

NJCC Standard Form of Tendering Questionnaire
· Application for Admission to Approved Lists of Contractors
· Application for Admission to Select Lists of Contractors for One Particular Contract

Building Contracts and Administration

TRADITIONAL PROCUREMENT

JCT Standard Form of Building Contract (JCT 80) in six versions

Supplements
· Fluctuations (two versions) and Formula Rules
· Sectional Completion (two versions)
· Contractor's Designed Portion (two versions)

Subcontracts
· Nominated SCs: NSC/T, NSC/A, NSC/N, NSC/W, NSC/C
· Domestic: DOM/1

JCT Intermediate Form of Building Contract (IFC 84)

Supplements
· Fluctuations (IFC/FS) and Formula Rules
· Sectional Completion (IFC/SCS)

Subcontracts
· Named SCs: NAM/T, NAM/SC
· Employer/Specialist Agreement: ESA/1
· Articles and Conditions for domestic: IN/SC

DESIGN AND BUILD PROCUREMENT

JCT Standard Form of Building Contract With Contractor's Design (WCD 81)

Subcontracts
· DOM/2 domestic subcontract Articles

JCT Agreement for Minor Works (MW 80)

JCT Agreement for Renovation Grant Works
· where an Architect/Contract Administrator is appointed (RG/A) 1994
· where no Architect/Contract Administrator is appointed (RG/C) 1994

JCT Standard Form of Prime Cost Contract (PCC 92)

Subcontracts
· Nominated SCs: NSC/T(PCC), NSC/C(PCC)

JCT Measured Term Contract (MTC 89)

JCT Jobbing Agreement Contract (JA/C 90)